ACCOLADES

"Tevis is a force to be reckoned with... When you meet with Tevis, whether one-on-one or in a group setting, she metaphorically holds a mirror to your self. You cannot escape. Whether it's the questions she asks, or her stories of clients embracing the challenges we relate to, it hits the spot."

—Daniel Goldfarb, *Bloomberg LP*

"Tevis provided me with the foundational structure needed to handle the challenges of becoming a CEO. Her unique ability to walk me through those challenges and opportunities both realized and future have prepared me for true, radical success."

—John Johnson, CEO, *Picture People*

"If you're ready to access the greatness within you, you've got the right book in your hands. As a client for many years, I can attest Tevis is the very best at transforming corporate cultures, engaging, invigorating and inspiring executives of every type to achieve their goals."

—Scott Andrews, *AOL* and *Millennial Media.*

"Truly "Game-Changing" guidance from someone who knows first-hand how to thrive while navigating corporate reality. No matter what your function, Tevis' incitement for achieving personally satisfying and sustainable success is absolutely achievable. From the champion of corporate mindfulness, Tevis packs lifetimes-worth of practical wisdom in this indispensable, accessible and wonderful book."

—Bernadette Brennan, *TV Azteca*

"Tevis inspires and amazes. Drawing from military service, leadership consulting and executive coaching, international business development, and strategy development, her approach is one of a marksman, wayward traveler, boardroom shark, constant dreamer, animal lover, occasional snowboarder, and sometimes surfer. There is no one more qualified to help you realize Radical Success."

—Manny Miravete, *Google*

"Tevis' process delivers next-level impact for professionals who want more! I have seen it in action in programs Tevis developed for me at White & Case and recommend it for anyone wanting to live at their highest levels of success and satisfaction."

—J. Kelly Hoey, Author *Build Your Dream Network,*
and *Angel Investor*

THE
GAME-CHANGER'S
GUIDE
TO
RADICAL
SUCCESS

THE
GAME-CHANGER'S
GUIDE
TO
RADICAL
SUCCESS

TEVIS ROSE TROWER

Contents

MANDALA OF CREATION

Our cover design features the Mandala of Creation, or Flower of Life, one of the most ancient and revered sacred images. Known to philosophers, architects and artists around the world, this design is considered a blueprint of life itself. References to this symbol have been found in drawings by Leonardo DaVinci, Kabbalah, places of worship in Galilee, and even in China's Forbidden City.

Opening with the Mandala here honors your connection to that unending process of transformation which permeates all systems.

Let it remind you that you are life in action, a creator.

Invocation

Most authors call this part of the book their "introduction." I prefer to call it an "invocation" because the process I'm about to share with you has less to do with introducing you to *me* than it does with introducing you to *yourself*. It's an invocation because Radical Success is all about calling forth, and getting to really know, *you*—your very best you.

You are going to play the biggest role in helping you to get more out of life. I'm assuming you want more out of life. I know I do. I'm so passionate about living as great a life as I am capable of, that I've made it my personal mission to figure out the best ways to go about doing so. I've also made it my life's work to help others to live their best lives too.

MY LIFE IS ALREADY PRETTY GOOD. IS THIS BOOK FOR ME?

This book is for people who have a pretty good life already, but find that, for some reason, they're still not truly fulfilled. Perhaps you figured out how to get a good education, which allowed you to participate in a respectable profession. You know how to keep a roof over your head, and have found your place within some sort of community, where you maintain decent relationships. You're happily married—or happily single. It's not as if you're walking around like an emotional zombie. But still, you want more. Just being "successful" isn't enough for you. The *more* you're looking for is what I call achieving your personal Optimal, your own definition of what can take your life from good to *great*.

Since 2002 I have worked with successful professionals to help them experience being Optimal. These people are the captains of industry at respected organizations including SAP, Google, Bloomberg, American Express, Disney, AOL, Yahoo!, Viacom, Chanel, and even the NYPD. Not unlike you, they'd mastered "having it all," but decided that wasn't good enough for them. Within whatever admirable life they had built, they decided they wanted more. They wanted to feel Optimal.

Game-Changing is the process I created for them. It isn't for everyone. It's not for people who are willing to settle for "good enough." It's not for people who deny having a desire for more. Owning that desire is key. Without desire to fuel you, you're not going to have the inner juice to change anything, least of all something as deeply ingrained as how you play the game of life. The mojo behind your own desire for more is what will help you identify specifically what you want. And just having it is proof that you're on the right track.

Put simply, if you're really the right kind of reader for this book (and it is the right kind of book for you) the following are true:

1. You already have a sense of accomplishment.

2. You want more.

If you can identify with these two conditions, then you're absolutely holding the right book. You're ready for Game-Changing. If you don't yet know what that means for yourself, don't worry. This book is designed to help you figure it out through a process that is less *self-help* and more *self-kickass*.No matter how much you've accomplished, like the thousands of accomplished professionals I've worked with, you suspect that you've got a lot more living to do. Despite the many trappings of success you acquire or skills you master, there is a longing inside of you to feel absolutely, vibrantly alive, consequential, and singular. You want to go from "keeping up" to "setting the pace." This inquietude is the root of all progress in life, all creativity, all innovation. This nagging longing is what propels you forward, makes you break with expectation and convention, and redefines life on your terms. It is connected to your inner truth.

MAKING FRIENDS WITH YOUR INNER TRUTH

Your inner truth is a key component in Game-Changing and achieving Radical Success. Sounds simple, right? Just be your self, and you can live life to the fullest. But identifying your inner truth, getting to know it, and incorporating it can be complicated. Often, there's resistance around letting it guide us.

There are a few reasons why:

1. Your inner truth doesn't necessarily conform to social norms. Examining it, living by it, and taking roads less traveled as a result can challenge your social safety net.

2. Honoring it can require letting go of the familiar comforts and experiences that have given you the closest approximation of happiness, because they stand in they way of things that can provide greater, more genuine happiness. But trading the familiar for the unknown is a leap of faith.

3. Brain chemistry. Those "to do" boxes we strive to check off throughout our lives often have little to do with our happiness or feeling truly connected with who we are, or with experiences that generate deep satisfaction. But each time we check one off, our sense of "satisfaction" and "happiness" gets reinforced chemically because our brains get a hit of dopamine. When fighting the fear of change—or of questioning our choices, or being different— we've also got a little opiate junkie inside our brains saying: "Why bother with all that discomfort when you can just get another hit if you ＿＿＿＿＿＿ (fill in the blank).

4. Aligning with our inner truth means abandoning all external authority and moving into an evaluative process where no one can tell us we "got it right." Think of all those Top 10 Tip articles—the reason publishing and media loves them, is that we love the

"good girl/boy" feeling we get by checking those boxes and getting them right. In our default search for someone to just tell us what to do, we confuse reading the checklist with actually accomplishing our desired outcomes. If there is no absolute authority, only experimentation and listening to outcomes, the experiment is never done, and by definition becomes a lifelong endeavor to watch, listen, try, and repeat. There's no way out of this if you are really going for Game-Changing. No one can tell you "you done good," because you become the ultimate authority. But our longing for validation is overpowering. And the fact that we get validation for external accomplishment in the form of compliments from others means that you not only get a dopamine hit from the act itself, you get another each time you impress people and receive those compliments.

Ideally, box checking is a variable ongoing timeline of *effort* to *done*, with hits of dopamine all along the way. Game-Changing is really for the rest of your life. We may sense this in some way, and the courage, character, and conviction required is one of a quiet power that roars within us when accessed.

We have two choices with regard to our inner truth: to be present to it and apply it, or to ignore it. Applying it may be scary and risky, but offers great dividends in the process. On the other hand, if you ignore it, not only does your life become dull, but also you lose your spark and the only horizon you see is one filled with more of the same.

Again, although your life as it is might be pretty good, you know that a better, stronger version is possible, one that's more authentic to you. Presencing yourself to inner truth is acknowledging your version of *great*. However you define your version, you want *great*. You can have *great*. And you should.

This personally defined *great* you're going for is contingent upon embracing a notion of *Radical Success*, and it is distinct from any keeping-up-with-the-Joneses checklist of success. Success, as society defines it, is largely about acquiring material goods or social status. For some it includes physical attractiveness, bank accounts, recognition, and countless idiosyncratic claims for bragging rights. You've already learned that game. Racking up more of those things just leads you toward more of the same.

Radical Success reaches beyond that. As an expression of your own version of "great," Radical Success includes whatever external stuff really matters to you, but it means you also master the ability to be profoundly engaged, and have an ongoing sense of being viscerally alive. Experiencing Radical Success means you first have to change your game. The life you've built is the result of learning and mastering the rules to some unspoken game. Given that you want more, you'll have to *up your game*, as they say, which means full-on living. Not just checking another box, but balls-to-the-wall going for it.

QUESTIONS TO LIVE BY

An important part of discovering your inner truth and the best life it can lead you to is asking yourself key questions. The Game-Change Process is built upon a foundation of ten questions. They're designed to plunge you into inquiry about your beliefs—about yourself and the nature of being alive—and to make real your own experience of Radical Success. You know these questions. They're the ones that keep you awake at night. You may never have uttered them, but you feel them lurking beneath your thoughts:

▶ **Am I living, or just existing?**

▶ **Is change possible?**

▶ **How do I begin?**

▶ **How much freedom and power do I have in creating my life?**

▶ **How will I know what to do?**

▶ **What actions will make my dreams a reality?**

▶ **What will happen if I fail?**

▶ **What if everyone thinks I'm crazy for doing this?**

▶ **How do I keep my faith?**

▶ **How do I sustain this way of being over time?**

There are countless options in life, and arguably more choices as you ascend the established ladders of success. Because of the breadth of possibilities, you are uniquely empowered to examine how your choices create your experiences. These ten questions and your well-considered answers to them will help you shift your position from *existing* to *living*, from *surviving* to *thriving*. In using them actively, you shift your efforts from endlessly pursuing false conditions for happiness to cultivating the experience of living fully. They are the secret to flourishing in a sustained Optimal state, rather than just getting by.

You'll use these ten questions as your guideposts throughout this process, though you can adapt them to fit your own vocabulary. Your own versions of these life questions may use different words, and take other forms, with subtle twists and meanings that ground the central idea of truth for you. Certainly your answers will be entirely your own. Essentially, life questions drive you to wonder what it means for you to be truly happy, and how to sustain that state through the wins and losses that are the essence of being alive.

As you immerse yourself, step-by-step, into this quest to learn how you take your proven ability to accomplish and repurpose it in support of the profound fulfillment of Radical Success, you'll see a couple of basic elements repeated throughout:

> ▶ **Chapters are each based upon one of these ten central questions. They serve as both organizing principles for the chapters, and as questions you ask yourself. Considering what I've got to say about the question provides only about 10 percent of the insight. The other 90 percent will come from asking yourself what you *really* think in response to each question, and integrating the resulting insights into how you live your life.**

▶ You're going to see sidebar invitations that are free-standing tools to help you get better at being fully present and aware – a requirement for experiencing an Optimal life. They may include awareness tools or breathing practices, or may ask you to jot something down. It's a good idea for you to practice these not only when you read the book, but also to then make it a point to integrate them into your daily life.

▶ You'll also see several charts, reflection areas where you can gain new insights about your own life, and conceptual diagrams to reinforce the information given. Where you see areas for you to write, make sure to do it. Where you see a chart, fill it in. Where you see a diagram, personalize it with the elements that reflect your own situation.

▶ Each chapter concludes with an Alignment Assignment. The Alignment Assignment is designed to help you gain insight into what it means to align with your unique version of Optimal, and to identify where, how, when, and why you don't. Each chapter's Alignment Assignment will require focused observation, not just on alignment, but lack of alignment in your own life and the world around you. Whether directing your attention externally or internally to various aspects of yourself, you'll be tasked with using your life experiences as the library and test lab for researching what you want, and knowing with crystal clarity what takes you closer to it and what doesn't. If you need more space to capture your thoughts, this process is all about giving yourself plenty of room to grow. Pull out a sheet of paper or napkin, and go for it.

MY PROMISE TO YOU

I keep the writing as straightforward as possible—as much like a heart-to-heart conversation as it can be. Leadership and personal development books tend to pack in countless footnoted references, case studies, and statistics in an attempt to earn your trust and suspend your disbelief. I'm going to resist the urge to illustrate every idea I share with such citations, client references, and percentages of outcomes. This is because your time and energy are precious and every word you read consumes both. Ideas can only excite you into action if they hold gravitas and inherent truth. If the content resonates, such references aren't necessary. If it doesn't, no amount of justification matters. (But if you're really interested in references, visit our website to see source information and examples of who we've worked with using this system.)

This system is the result of study and testing. Because human longing for meaning and fulfillment is as old as recorded history, this book is transparently influenced by many traditions and concepts, such as Judeo-Christian ideas, Eastern traditions, wisdom gleaned from the Renaissance, as well as lessons learned from the scientific and industrial revolutions. It is spiced with insights developed from watching how the media and technology influence our ideas of who we are. It is validated by advances in neuroscience and all the disciplines devoted to your evolving understanding of what it means to exist. To bring all this together, I've had some great guides along the way, starting with intrepid teachers who nurtured me through Montessori school as a child, and followed by many wise, renegade mentors throughout my formal education. I worked on the practical application of living well in corporate, social, and philanthropic arenas with support from both world-renowned and completely unknown yogis, Buddhist teachers, coaches, and gurus. Generous as it is, life has served up plenty of lessons along the way.

You will get the most out of this book by taking your time with it. It is deceptively short, but don't gulp it down too quickly. Make the decision to digest these ideas slowly. Let each chapter influence your consciousness between readings. Studies show we increasingly skim through books, get some cool ideas, but quickly move on, life pretty unchanged by the entire process. But Game-Change requires some marinating in order for you to reap the full effect. If you rush, the power of your conditioned, discursive mind might prevent you from honestly examining what is keeping your life exactly as it is right now.

If you're already really happy, empowered, moving toward personal and professional goals, highly energized, sleeping well, eating sustainably, loving your body, creatively expressing yourself, financially harmonious, and in a positive relationship with others and the world around you, use this process to give yourself a cosmic whack in the head to take yourself to an even higher level of fulfillment—because you need one from time to time.

If you're unsure why you have this book in your hands, why someone gave it to you, or why you acted on that odd urge to buy it, sit back for a second and ask yourself: *What if crossing the gap between how I am and how I wish to be is as simple as wanting to make that leap badly enough that I'm willing to begin experimenting with my life? To risk believing that what I already have isn't all that's possible?* If there's a part of you that wants to nudge forward, then keep reading.

You can use this process to improve <u>any</u> area of life. It's been applied to a variety of situations by constituencies as disparate as survivors of 9/11 overcoming the deaths of loved ones to executives desiring weight loss, from the struggle to maintain passion for work to the longing to ignite passion in the bedroom. You will achieve the biggest results by deeply absorbing the process, actively applying the concepts while you're reading, and then continuing to work the insights through every aspect of life. That's right—*every* aspect, again and again, over time, but especially whenever you recognize that you have dead-ended, stopped thriving, lost your mojo, or moved into conflict with others.

This material will prompt new insights about *yourself*. Treasure them! This book is intended to support a conversation between you and yourself. Savoring the process will help you keep it your own, and that's where the payoff lies. Don't worry about other people's opinions, and definitely don't seek them out. Really, it's no one else's business to agree or disagree with what you will discover about yourself or the decisions you will make as a result. While you're diving into this heady mix of ideas, inquiries, and actions, remember that not everyone around you is engaging in the significant shifts you are taking on.

Which gives rise to a note of caution: If we're viewing life as a journey, it's important to recognize that not everyone is on the same bus. As you learn to tease out what moves you forward and what keeps you stuck, what serves your greatest good and what strangles it into stagnation, you may notice that there are people around you who aren't so comfortable with the changes you're making in how you think, what you talk about, and what you do with any given moment on the planet. You may also notice that you're not as comfortable with people, conversations, and activities that you used to engage in as if on cruise control. What once felt normal may begin to feel awkward. Engaging in autopilot conversations may become stifling. Take heart! If you persisted in being as you have always been, the process would not work and you'd get what you've always gotten—perhaps a life that is good enough, but not one that allows you to feel fully alive. Those awkward moments are a sign that you're learning and growing.

Give the people around you permission to feel uncomfortable, just as you give yourself permission to fly in the face of their expectations. Try to do so without labeling everyone around you as *wrong* or thinking that somehow because you signed up for optimizing your life, everyone else should, too. There may be friends with whom you share this process, but it would be better for your relationship if you let them wrestle with the ideas in this book on their own, rather than attempting to teach them and muddy your friendship.

Intentional change must be cultivated, and Game-Change is not a passive experience but one of active engagement by you with your own life.

Let's begin.

Part 1

PRE-GAME PLANNING

Chapter 1

AM I LIVING OR JUST EXISTING?

Dare to ask, and answer honestly. If you've done pretty well in life already, then clearly you know how to seek fulfillment. This might mean you've collected the right combination of V's, S's, P's, or even C's after your name on your business card. It might mean you've created the configuration of family you want, you're living in a home that you truly aspired to own, and you travel according to your sense of curiosity or reward. It likely also means you command a degree of responsibility that's not only evidence you possess the requisite skills, but that you've also earned the respect of others.

But even with all you have, and have accomplished, are you living life at your very best? (OR in the best way possible? At your very best...not sure about) Are you Optimal in all you do? Are you truly thriving and fulfilled? To what level are you personally engaged with everything in your life? Your level of personal engagement is key to your fulfillment. For many, engagement is the hardest thing to establish and maintain. But that's not cause for regret: It's an invitation to assess and take action. A different kind of action.

All the achievements in your life have required a certain kind of action. They've required a hunger and drive on your part. You've had to be disciplined and attentive. Living Optimally requires those things, too, but it also requires something else: the courage to gamble big.

Optimal is the state you experience when you consistently align your thoughts, words, and actions in support of the life you want. It depends on resolute rejection of the notion that what you currently have in your life is all that's possible—even if, in the eyes of others, what you already have seems pretty good. It means being greedy with life itself, unyielding in your choices, actions, and ways of being that make you feel vibrantly alive. Game-Changing in support of an Optimal life requires all of that achievement you've created for yourself *and* attending to your quality of experience. It means shifting focus from simply achieving benchmark accomplishments, to sustaining a deep, radical experience of success that is true to your deepest longing. It's having the beach house if that's what you want, but also feeling supremely alive in it.

A TIME-HONORED QUEST

That you want this type of something more for yourself isn't to be downplayed or dismissed. It's nothing to be embarrassed or demure about. It's been a topic of fascination for influential thinkers throughout history. Countless traditions maintain that realizing this longing for fulfillment, for more, is actually the point of being alive. The *kosha* system in Hindu philosophy is one of the many models from Eastern traditions that demonstrate how earnestly addressing your longing for fundamental happiness is your ultimate challenge and point of evolution. It says you are made up of five layers (*koshas*), each with their own distinct function and organized in this order: physical, energetic, mental, wisdom, and finally, way on the inside, the essential self. While your survival focus is to attend to the most tangible needs, it is not until the most subtle, essential self is expressed through all those layers that your life is complete. The word for the most inner layer? *Ananda* – which is Sanskrit for *bliss*.

These kinds of ideas aren't limited to eastern thinkers. They appear in western traditions, too. From the Greeks, we get a word you might use every day without realizing its root meaning. We use the word *enthusiasm* broadly to express positive emotion for anything from puppies to winning the big game, but its foundation is *en THEOS* – full of the spirit of God. From the Romans, we get the Latin-derived word *inspired*, the most basic translation of which is *full of spirit*, breath, or life.

It's not just ancient sages who say true success is an inside job. Contemporary thinkers also offer ample theories as to how all this works. In 1943, American psychologist Abraham Maslow studied the top one percent of society to arrive at his theory that once our physical and social needs are met, and we feel safe and good about ourselves, we then face the ultimate challenge: actualizing Self, or who we really are. Maslow is not alone in this line of thinking. University of Chicago Psychologist Mihaly Csikszentmihalyi makes the case that happiness isn't so much about how much stuff you have or what your profession is. He says cultivating absolute engagement and mental absorption is the condition for Optimal experience. University of Pennsylvania Professor Martin Seligman's work on positive psychology has resulted in volumes of content and practices that are shown to help you be more present, engaged, and fulfilled in your life, and none of it has anything to do with your job title, marital status, zip code, or whether you like your boss. So, no matter what you've already accomplished in your life, there are countless voices of wisdom urging you to get on with addressing the transcendent question of what will actually make you happy.

"Radical Success" is an expression that encapsulates this concept of maintaining profound happiness in the midst of living an externally successful life. It is different from success as evaluated through the eyes of the outside world. It comes from the root of your being, and exists irrespective of moderation or appraisal by others. Unlike the relative success you have been taught to value above all else, Radical Success is fundamental to who you truly are, and is inextricably tied to the success of being who you are in all you do. It bears comparison to no one, because it is grounded in your individual truth.

Some exemplars of Radical Success are Steve Jobs, Thomas Edison, Albert Einstein, Elizabeth Warren, Twyla Tharpe, Galileo, Leonardo DaVinci, Shakespeare, great artists, musicians, risk-takers, inventors and creators of every type and stripe. These Game-Changing individuals and countless others like them move into their respective arenas with a passion for what they do. But it's more than just that. They've also cultivated a deep relationship with who they are. The game they play is not one of conformity, comfort, or currying favor. Their *modus operandi* is purely focused on the precious and solitary task of being fully alive as themselves. Just consider the breathtaking results. To achieve such a level of self-expression and Radical Success, you must first examine your own life for insights as to what you're creating – and want to create – out of the experience of being alive.

I HAVE ASKED MYSELF THESE QUESTIONS, TOO

When it comes to assessing the connection between accomplishment and fulfillment, I can offer my own life as a ready example. At the height of my career as a corporate strategist and dealmaker, I had an impressive job title and an enviable Manhattan apartment, and enjoyed the satisfaction of real organizational responsibility. I vacationed around the globe, and was blessed with many wonderful relationships with friends and family, including a romantic partnership that kept me warm at night with commitment and children on the horizon. I carried not a cent of debt and was steadily building assets. By most standards, I'd made it. I "had it all." What else could I want?

A lot, actually. But I couldn't put a name to it. I found myself experiencing a state I can best describe as *yearning*. At times I attributed this profound disquietude to external issues and outcomes beyond my control. If a friend had managed to drag out of me what was really on my mind, my knee-jerk responses might have begun with the words: "If only so and so would..." or "When such and such finally..." But as quickly as one external complaint was resolved, my discontent would morph and resurface through another expression, another focal point of festering. I was deeply discontented, yet unsure of whatever it was for which I longed.

I did what most of us do in the face of unhappiness—I tried to bury it. I ran from it. I diluted it with alcohol. I did everything I could think of to soothe my ache: had sex, shopped in fine boutiques, lined up bigger business deals, hosted creative parties, took up cooler hobbies, made new friends, reconnected with old friends, went on fancier vacations, spent time with family, avoided time with family, engaged in volunteer activities, and, when all that failed, meditated. No matter what I did, after the Saks bill was paid, *savasana* was over, or the hangover passed, the ache was still there. I was successful, but I wasn't content. So I surrendered, and started to listen to my inner voice.

Dogged attention to my thoughts showed me that although I was working myself into a frenzy to make sure I had all the elements of a successful life, in my head I was constantly finding fault with my life. With all that energy spent achieving and so many fruits to show for it, why the incessant fixation on everything that *wasn't* okay? While notching up the ladder of achievements, I'd spent no time cultivating my own happiness.

By charting my satisfaction relative to the little losses and wins embedded in the course of a day or week, I was able to see there wasn't much of a correlation between attainment and contentment. My state-of-being apparently depended very little upon external variables such as projects under way, financial security, or how well I was relating with others. While that would be a positive statement if I meant to convey that I was simply so happy that nothing could dim my disposition, quite the opposite was true. Nothing seemed to sustainably brighten it. Though I was far from depressed, any sense of deep satisfaction I achieved was momentary at best. Despite all of the moving, shaking, and schmoozing I was doing professionally and socially, I couldn't evade the suspicion that fulfillment must be about something *more*. Once any high from accomplishments inevitably yielded to discontentment, with great efficiency I'd simply distract myself by plotting my next "win." Looking around, it was evident that a majority of other people I observed were wrestling the same nameless, faceless demons, no matter how much they "succeeded."

Demon number one? The habit of discontent. When we confuse relative success with fulfillment, we live in a constant state of finding fault with the world around us, because that helps us to identify new potential sources of relief, or comfort. As with any other bad habit like this, it begins to generate discontent from within. Over time, habitually projecting discontent onto the external world inherently defines our experience.

Recognizing this, I began to wonder how to more actively craft not only perceptions, but also experiences and outcomes. I began to wonder how to create a new relationship with this ache, harnessing its energy to drive towards greater satisfaction. It was clear that my life offered plenty of evidence of my ability to effectively navigate toward my goals. Why not use that same power to figure out what is fundamentally true about *me*. What supports my own state of contentment? With little more than incessant curiosity and the influence of great teachers from various philosophical, leadership, and psychological traditions to guide me, I took a risk and acted upon my desire to uncover and experience an Optimal state of being.

My curiosity became a quest for going beyond living a life that is "good enough" to experiencing a Radical Success that is far more than attainment of any material or accomplishment goals I might have once assigned myself. In the endeavor to be my very best, my Optimal self, I had to see where my own perceptions got in the way of my fulfillment in life, and superimposed a false limitation on my ability to choose and act freely in support of that fulfillment. It was a gamble, one that required me to question every conviction I've ever had about what it is to be "Tevis." I did it on faith that the outcome would be worth the effort. And has it ever.

Through this process I've overcome mammoth self-imposed limitations and considerable external challenges. It enabled me to bootstrap a start-up business into a multimillion-dollar international organization, doing so in the midst of our nation's most staggering economic downturn, and without any outside investment. It showed me how to cultivate forgiveness and loving dialogue with every member of my family. It allowed me to peacefully exit a very difficult marriage, to reclaim my sexuality and embrace intimacy, to establish leadership in the competitive worlds of both business and yoga, and ultimately, to land solidly on my feet, Optimal every single day.

Applying these insights, I've worked with Fortune
500 companies on issues of engagement, purpose, and
passion, capturing what works and canning what doesn't.
The result of this endeavor is the Game-Change Process—
powerful tools and insights into how you can create a life
of your conscious choosing and achieve ultimate satisfaction. I've shared these realizations with thousands of
intelligent, hard-working professionals who aspire to be
their very best selves, just like you and me.

POWER PAUSE

The next time you find yourself with an unplanned pause, practice
noticing your well-being. In traffic, waiting for an elevator, waiting
for a meeting to start, instead of grabbing for your phone to
check messages or attend to business, try this: Relax your body
into whatever position you are in (sitting, standing, etc.). Scan
your body from the soles of your feet, up through your legs and
hips. Continuing upward, as you notice your belly, watch for an
unhurried breath rhythm. Relax your shoulders, neck,

Like any good hostess, I'll share a few words about
myself. I straddle worlds easily. I'm the kid with a stutter
who grew up to be an acclaimed public speaker. I'm the
hippie girl who joined the U.S. Army, then saved every
dime I had so I could go do grassroots development work
in impoverished communities in Central America. I'm the
philosophical seeker who is savvy in money matters, so
went to America's top master's degree program in international business. I'm the former marketer who was both
fascinated by *and* conflicted ideologically with the process

of selling carbonated sugar water to little kids around the planet. I'm the friend who talks to anyone from any social class, race, religion, or walk of life, because I haven't met anyone yet who *doesn't* have a lesson or two to share.

The ideas in this book have been road-tested on both the most and least receptive audiences. In my work collaborating with corporations (and quite a few amazing non-corporate organizations), I craft and deliver strategies and programs to ensure there are happier, healthier, more engaged folks walking through the office doors each day. Corporations care about this. The savviest among them will invest in it, because they know human assets represent over 75 percent of their market value. As advances in medicine, neuroscience, leadership science, and even actuarial information improve our ability to measure correlations among mindset, self-care, productivity, health claims, and effective leadership, organizations are becoming acutely aware that the effectiveness of the organization is directly impacted by employees' state of mind, behavior, and self-care.

CULTIVATING CALM

Notice your thoughts. Are they rushed and hurried? Is the content fixed on times past or yet to come? Shift entirely into acknowledging that in this moment you are absolutely fine. Using the Power Pause as a base, add these words to your mental activity as you watch your breath: With each inhale, think "calm," and with each exhale, think "peace."

My clients have included amazing best-in-class companies such as Google, Viacom, AOL, Disney, American

Express, and Bloomberg, as well as many organizations striving to emulate them. I've built leadership experiences for high-performing attorneys at leading law firms such as White & Case, Cleary Gottleib, and Meyer-Brown. In the depths of the economic downturn, I hurled a dry-eraser just over the heads of sixty or so Morgan Stanley directors to make a point about the function of fear. When Chanel needed to thaw chilly attitudes among their boutique staff, they sent me across the country to talk about the power of embodying luxury. When the New York City Police Department wanted to show 300 police officers how to master their stress response, I reported for duty.

The book you hold wasn't developed in a vacuum—rather, it was derived from serving these amazing organizations. I devised the Game-Changing Process by addressing employee engagement and performance issues across hundreds of thousands of employees, with all their varied professional and life situations, and their assorted interpersonal and logistical constraints. There is no pat formula or format. This process is a perspective shift I myself needed, then adapted and applied with clients. It's something I continue to see results from, both in my own life and in the lives of the hundreds of corporate professionals I work with at any given moment. All of this began with that initial question: Am I really living, or just existing? Like the sages throughout time have exhorted: This is what you now must ask yourself.

Be as great as you can be. That's my invitation to you, because living fully is more accessible than you think. Whether you go for it by Game-Changing or walking down some other wisdom path, please do it. Now.

Alignment Assignment

LIVING/EXISTING SELF-ASSESSMENT

1. At the end of each day, before you go to sleep, perform a review of the day and note any moments in which you felt fulfilled, really alive. Re-live them by playing them back in your mind.

2. As you walk through your week, notice how you talk about your life – your day, your week. Are your words enthusiastic?

3. After each conversation you have over the next 24 hours, rate your level of overall contentment in the content, sentiment, your word selection, and your tone of voice. How receptive are you to what unfolds?

4. Give yourself a 5-minute observation practice. Sit somewhere quietly with a timer set, eyes open with a soft focus, and allow your thoughts to flow freely. What is the content of your thoughts? Is it positive? Is it negative? How would you describe what's going on in there?

Chapter 2

IS CHANGE POSSIBLE?

Over dinner one night a friend said, with snarky pessimism, that for the most part all change is temporary. To use her words, "Same whore...different dress." Maybe you've had similar philosophical soccer matches with friends, knocking this question around. Get ready, because Game-Change is a personal life-change World Cup. While considering the nuances of "real" change vs. superficial change, you begin the immersion in your own Optimal state of being with this quick question: *Can you decide you believe change is possible?* You'd better, or you won't get off the couch.

I sincerely believe real change is possible because life is nothing if not change. I also believe choosing your changes can be as profound and lasting as you want it to be. Nothing is as critical to your ability to create positive change for yourself as your belief in it. If you're not quite there yet, if you need proof, you can be your own guinea pig. You are your best test subject for the possibility of positive change and your ability to affect it.

You can become an expert on your ability to change

by studying evolution—your own, and even of people around you. The best evidence of real change is the progress you can see in your own life. Once upon a time you couldn't walk, read, understand language, or speak. There was a time when your educational goals may have seemed like monumental challenges. Now they are an unconscious part of who you are. However distant any job or home or lover or anything else you've attained may have seemed at one point, you strived to achieve it, and change occurred. Among all your personal examples of pursing change, there are countless instances of success. Name them. Become an expert on all the ways you've made changes happen in your life.

Using this table, write down some of those examples. This will help to make the evidence more concrete:

Age Range	Accomplishment	Obstacle
0-5 years old		
6-16 years old		
17-25 years old		
26-35 years old		
36-50 years old		
50+ years old		

Okay, now you've demonstrated for yourself that you can be an agent of change in your life. You've recalled instances from the past where you achieved new benchmarks, which allowed you to tell yourself and the world, "Hey, I made it!" You know, without a doubt, that you can affect change. Now you have to decide what kinds of change you most want to see in your life – and, if you want Radical Success, choose some different kinds and approaches.

What kind of change is *worth* pursuing? What different things and circumstances are worth having? If you want to experience deep fulfillment in your own life, you have to think about Game-Changing—literally retooling the rules you give yourself for going about your life.

A Game-Changer is a visionary, a creator of new paradigms. Investment dictionaries describe a Game-Changer as one who has new and different ideas that stand out from the crowd. Slang dictionaries say a Game-Changer *radically changes a situation*, whether we're talking about a person, an idea, or an event. Considered organizationally, a Game-Changer occurs when a visionary strategist uses creative innovation to evolve existing business plans, or conceives of an entirely new plan with new considerations and perspectives. Sounds pretty exciting, right? Can you think of people who do this? Putting it bluntly, like the oxygen mask you administer in mid-flight emergencies: What you want to give to the world, you must always first give to yourself. You want to be a visionary? You have to cultivate vision. You want to Game-Change? You have to Game-Change your life.

What does Game-Changing look like for you? What will you change so that you can slide up the fulfillment gage to Optimal? It should be as unique as your fingerprints.

There is no one-size-fits-all formula for achieving fulfillment in life. No magazine article or expert-formulated checklist can define what you should change in order to go from torpor to thriving. Optimal varies from person to person and moment to moment. Your desired outcomes are related to who you are, personally and demographically, and what you're navigating in your life, whether it's a turbulent work situation, or the demands of parenting and commuting, or a new chapter in a personal relationship.

When I first started supporting people in optimizing their lives, I wondered whether I could identify some standard factor that would allow any and all clients to craft a life that supports a creative essence and clarity. I discovered that, as a constant, you must first look to an obvious dissatisfaction within some aspect of your life – career, relationships, health, fiscal fitness, overall enjoyment – as indicators of action needed. But these vary from person to person. Working with a variety of people, who represent a wide variety of work situations, diverse demographic factors, and countless personality variables, it became clear: There is no one formula for having a fulfilled life.

If I couldn't find one set of variables that would guarantee this Optimal state from one person to the next, I wanted to identify the factors that determine the difference between true success and a nice try. I wondered what strategies or factors make change effective and lasting, no matter what that desired change may be. After all, if you're going for aligning with what is radically grounded in who

TEVIS ROSE TROWER

you are, you'd better make sure you have elements in place to keep you on target, and training wheels of sorts to keep you moving along. As I couldn't find studies that identify life alignment success (yet!), I looked for common themes in studies identifying the differentiators between people who persisted in any desired life changes, and people who made changes in the short term and then boomeranged back to the status quo...or worse.

As I aggregated findings across various studies, from weight loss to increased earnings to quitting smoking, a few major themes emerged. I'll go into more detail in a moment and throughout this guide, but here is the short list of the most important actions to take in order to sustain change, as cited by people who have done so:

▶ **Cultivate a new self-image.**

▶ **Set specific goals.**

▶ **Measure your actions.**

▶ **Practice selective attention.**

▶ **Cultivate faith.**

▶ **Question your conditioned responses.**

▶ **Become a learner.**

▶ **Get competitive.**

▶ **Establish or build a community of support.**

▶ **Keep going no matter what.**

Seem like no-brainers? On the whole, I've found most people can rally around this list. People who are interested in taking life to the next level, in being Optimal, can usually agree with most of them, if not all, as being critical drivers of Radical Success. Chances are, as you examine evidence of your ability to change, you can credit your success to a combination of these practices.

You can't, however, stop at simple agreement with this list and expect results. Intentional change is not a spectator sport. Expecting change to happen because you think that how other people did it makes sense and would work for you is just an evasive tactic - w*oulda, coulda, shoulda*. For this process to work, you have to personalize and internalize these elements, defining what each practice means to you, and then commit to using them. Think of it this way: You wouldn't set out on an expedition to climb Mt. Everest without identifying and thoroughly understanding the tools you need. Once you made your shopping list, you'd go out and get your own set.

Let's dive in to what each factor of lasting success really means. You're going to see very quickly how both idiosyncratic and interconnected they are.

Cultivate a new self-image. You have to get "sick and tired of being sick and tired," says Red Hot Chili Peppers front man Anthony Kiedis, a self-described addict in recovery, perhaps quoting AA. Whoever first came up with the phrase was right. Don't like being tired, over-tasked, stressed? Change your idea of yourself into that of one who allows enough time to accomplish what is necessary. Sick of being the one afraid to speak up in a group? Change your image of yourself into that of one who contributes thoughtfully. Feel limited in your creativity? Decide you are someone who pays attention to, and cultivates, new ideas. You have to become so disenchanted with the self you've cultivated to date that there is no realistic alternative but to dedicate yourself fully to figuring out who you really want to be, and how you really want to be. Again, this means you also have to have courage enough to admit to *wanting more*. You have to fall in love, not just with the idea of having more energy or a powerful title or whatever else you want, but with all the aspects involved in being that person who is peaceful, driven, enthusiastic, healthful, passionate, playful or whatever else you really want to experience (of yourself?) in this lifetime. You have to first imagine a state of being that will be the most satisfying state possible. By doing that, and then continuing with the subsequent important actions on the list above, you'll acquire the rest of the tools you need to dedicate your mind, body, soul, and actions to being that person *now*.

Set specific goals. Once you name the true version of yourself you wish to experience being, you must identify goals, your progress toward which will serve as indicators of your successful alignment. Be clear, however, that goals are not all the same—there are outcome goals and there are process goals, and you need BOTH to be successful. Outcome goals will imply finality, and prompt a response of "Yay, I did it! Crack the champagne, let's party!" when they are achieved. Having your first photography exhibit, winning a board seat, losing twenty pounds—in all of these examples, there is a final *hurrah* moment. On the other hand, process goals answer the question, "What are you doing along the way?" Whether it's noting, "I will work out for at least thirty minutes a day," or, "I will give myself ten minutes of downtime to simply breathe before and after work," process goals are what allow the metamorphosis to unfold. They incorporate taking actions repeatedly over time, and represent either new activities or new levels of commitment necessary to achieve your outcome goals.

IF AT FIRST YOU'RE NOT UNCOMFORTABLE ... YOU'RE DOING IT WRONG

When you think of a new idea of self, you need to identify both outcomes and processes that will make that new self a reality. An outcome goal should be set high enough that the process you use to achieve it will feel new and uncomfortable. Yes, that's right. I'm suggesting it is to your advantage to take yourself out of your comfort zone here. Here's where the sting comes from: Naming outcome goals is a bit like confessing your dreams, the ones you've always thought were beyond your reach, or that others would disapprove of. Identifying process goals forces you to confront how you get in the way of your own dreams. Fortunately, this puts you on the road to achieving them anyway. As you repeat the process goals you've designated, you create a new "normal" for yourself. Over time these process goals feel organic, and as you use them to experience change, these actions begin to change you. As you attain your outcomes and continue to set new outcome goals, the old outcomes begin to look like mile markers along your path. The repeated commitment to both types of goals is the "special sauce" ingredient needed to make change happen—each time you fulfill your process and outcome commitments, you come closer to actually being who you want to be.

Measure your actions – often! If you have any doubts at all that you are making progress, you can easily prove it to yourself this way: by measuring your actions. Once you've named your goals, you have to measure what you're actually doing, how much of it you're doing, how often, and what you experience as a result. This may mean creating a measurement mechanism to reflect what you want and how much closer you're getting to it – a daily log, a regular check-in call with a supportive friend, an online tracking tool, etc. For some, it will mean engaging in routine reflection time, looking at the day behind you and planning for the days ahead. Or it could be more literal, such as counting calories ingested and burned. It can mean recording or "logging" how you spend time, how much water/alcohol you drink, or what time you go to bed and what time you get up. Equally impactful, be sure to note how each of these actions *makes you feel*. Whatever the goal is, whether measured with pen and paper or pixel alone, you must have a measurement element embedded in your process to mitigate the tendency to backslide toward complacency.

Studies of all types of tracking and logging have shown that there is usually a gap between what you *think* you are doing with your life and choices, and what you are *actually* doing. For example, in one immersion I teach, the executives who are chosen to participate routinely cite lack of time as the cause of their inaction in support of their desired outcomes. Because of this they are asked to log how they spend their time, and to the last person, they realize they spend time needlessly on voluntary actions that in no way support their stated goals. This time-clutter can easily go undetected. Uncovering it through the measurement mechanism of keeping a time/activity log reveals to participants just how much their life and subsequent choices actually are within their control – instant power!

Measurement works for both process goals and outcome goals, so pay close attention and log whatever actions you take—yes, even when you take counterproductive ones. Whether your goal is as specific as a health metric, or as generalized as career advancement or passion in your love relationship, you can very easily keep track of lifestyle choices that align with your goal. Many people attempting to make changes in their lives lament the slow speed of attainment—the agony of the process. The measurement element in these moments is your ability to catch your *thoughts*. Generally, the voice telling you to backslide on your goals is the conditioned voice that is not aligned with your deeper idea of your defined Optimal.

Practice selective attention—choose what messages you feed your brain. The most important thing for you to watch is what you feed your brain. When it comes to brain food, you are what you eat. There are going to be people around you who support you in whatever you want to change, and there are going to be people who are uncomfortable with it. In addition, plenty of people around you may fall into a gray area, both supporting it and expressing discomfort with it. Because your thinking is formed largely in response to shared values, you will experience many messages that conflict with the changes you want to make. You're going to hear people pander to the norm and expect you to do so, as well. You're going to hear plenty of messages about why what you're taking on is foolish, doomed, or a waste of time. Well-meaning loved ones will tease you with a chuckle for precisely the harmless action that most deeply serves you, but terrifies them. This goes for media messages, as well. The challenge is to always choose what you listen to, and choose how you listen to it. As you hear people expressing negative messages, listen for the motivation beneath each speaker's words. For example, getting jollied out of going to your guitar lesson in favor of yet another round of cocktails with the guys isn't going to support your goal of integrating learning, music, and fun into your life. As you hear that sort of message from well-intentioned pals, rather than either succumbing to it or resenting them for it, try to hear it with the affection from which it emanates, and go to your class anyway. This includes outright naysaying as well. If you hear anecdotes relating how someone else's efforts for change or a break with the norm were total folly, listen for your heart breaking at the thought of your own failure, and decide you'll stay the course anyway.

People will innocently and easily use negative humor, factoids, and examples aplenty to try to get you to change back to how you have been in the past. Don't let their fear impinge your resolve. Your courage to change is an inadvertent and uncomfortable mirror that forces them to look at their own lives and choices. Listen wisely, and remember that you have the power to decide what messages you're willing to take in, and take to heart. Determine that the messages you ultimately receive will only be those that reinforce your resolve to be who you want to be. That determining power is wholly yours. It's at the root of how you interpret the opinions and input of others.

A final note about messages from unsupportive messengers: Whether they know not what they do or are completely aware of attempting to sabotage your resolve, forgive them in your heart and stay your course.

Cultivate faith. Put yourself on a steady diet of inspiration, whether derived from belief in a supreme power or from someone else's success story. Stories are a great source of inspiration, and the best stories are those that touch your heart, maybe make you feel a little burn in the corners of your eyes, or a sublime tightness at the back of your throat. Strong physical responses to inspirational stories defy the rational, calm reserve of your discursive mind, and serve as a powerful antidote to any naysaying voices you might hear around you or even in your own mind. Allegories of success – whether from the world of sports, or history, or from people in our own lives – are testaments to the possibility of change and its accessibility to everyone. Savor these examples and be attentive to any form of inspiration that triggers physical and emotional response. Use them to remind yourself of your own ability to achieve.

Question your conditioned responses. Most people have a long list of a + b = c equations functioning as the autopilot force that keeps their lives exactly as they are. These conditioned behaviors and the assumptions that underlie them are major sources of sabotage. Each time you take an action, remind yourself of what you want, and make yourself take the action that will best align you with it. Are you always the "yes" person, accepting responsibilities and commitments despite the cost to your energy, attitude, and self-respect? Respectfully say "no" instead, and see what happens. Feeling sluggish after work? Snacking, napping, or drinking is just going to take that energy even further down—you need to inject power into your body and mind. Get up and take a brisk walk instead. Is staring at your computer making you feel brain-dead? You don't need a snack or distraction, you need a stimulus—go stretch or walk some stairs. Feeling edgy after a long day? Slamming your system with toxic amounts of alcohol is a cruel choice with psycho-emotional boomerang effects. Regardless of your historic knee-jerk response to the stimulus life serves up, you've got a choice. In those moments, objectively assess your current state, consider what will take you from there to your Optimal state, and then *do* it. Intercept your sleepwalking, resist your conditioned urge, and take empowered action instead. Each time you do this, you connect to your own power. Game-Change is about taking deliberate action, not about operating on autopilot.

Become a learner. A major indicator of your ability to cultivate happiness is your dedication to lifelong learning. As an adult, you become addicted to the confidence of knowing what you're doing, and so discomfort might arise when you find yourself faced with a new experience, in which you don't know what you're doing. You must embrace the discomfort that comes with doing new things. Unfortunately, you can't travel the full distance to Radical Success fueled only with the things you already know, housed in the places where you already look for answers. If you could, you'd already be living as you truly long to live. Aside from the experiential gains and discoveries you make by learning new skills and trying new activities, the process of learning itself releases happy chemicals in your body, like dopamine, serotonin, and other endorphins, clarifying your mind, increasing resiliency and creativity, and boosting your mood. The neurological effect of consuming the *new* is that you affirm and align with the ever-changing nature of the universe by expanding your own little world. Study a language. Take up tai chi. Learn to sing. Whatever it is that's new for you, let go of your addiction to the feelings associated with knowing it all, and allow yourself to instead warm up to the discomfort that hangs around the gateway to learning something new. As you do so, that discomfort will lose its power over you. Whatever topic or skill you can think of learning about – perhaps something you've never given yourself permission to try – get started on it, and it will be a powerful antidote to stagnation.

Get competitive. Whether it's a friendly wager with a colleague, or entering an actual judged event, the spirit of competition is one of intention, commitment, effort, and measured outcome, all of which can powerfully support you in achieving Radical Success. If you know yourself to be inspired by being competitive, or you like the notion of a good old-fashioned wager with a friend – or even with yourself – dig in and go for the gold!

Establish or build a community of support. Because not everyone in your life might understand the changes you are making, it can be important to find people who are willing to stand alongside you, cheering you on. Tell those people what you're up to, and ask them to lend their energetic and emotional support. Whether you want this support to be active or just in "vibe" form, knowing there are people out there who are rooting for you can make a big difference in your process and outcomes. Be public about your longing for change. You may be surprised to find others who long for changes themselves. And, who knows, your example may just give *them* the courage to act on this feeling themselves. If you can't find such people in your immediate social circle, a support group can be a great resource. Chances are, these days you can easily find one online.

Keep going no matter what. What happens if you make missteps, or suffer setbacks that are beyond your control? For many of us, it's so easy to see these as justification for giving up on the journey. The truest indicator of success is your ability to be stubborn about your goals in the face of the temptation to surrender. So you blew a day or two, maybe even a week or month. Perhaps an entire year will pass without you making progress toward your goal. Let's face it, if you had given up on every goal you've ever had, chances are you wouldn't be the person you are today. Reflect back on the challenges you've faced in your life that provide evidence of your ability to achieve—to stand strong. No matter how much time has passed between the moment of recognition and your last aligned action, re-envision your objective and stick with it. Do not sell short your dreams, nor your ability to fulfill them.

THE TEN FACTORS OF SUCCESS AT WORK:
A CASE STUDY

I know these ten factors of success to be key because I've witnessed them in action within many clients' change processes. Take "James" for example.

As standing Vice President of Sales for four successful years, James badly wanted to be named Chief Executive Officer. He had both the operational chops and the relationships to really succeed in that position. It was clear to him that he needed to improve relationships within the company in order to win this promotion; input from performance evaluations told him others were confused by the way he interacted with people, being too "buddy-buddy" with people in an overly familiar way, while often also coming off as an alienating know-it-all. What's more, his boss, the departing CEO, didn't trust that James' casual demeanor conveyed the gravitas necessary to win the support of the venture capitalists who owned the company and controlled the board. Despite his personal conviction that James was the right man for the job, he knew only James could convince the board of his talent, and only after making certain changes.

In moving towards his goal of winning the CEO spot, James knew he'd have to do more than simply make a business case, show results, and go present to the board. In a world that tells you everything is all about the numbers, trust me, James' numbers were great. But in this, as in many cases, it wasn't just about the numbers. These VC guys sitting in Connecticut needed to feel for themselves that James qualitatively represented the man they wanted at the helm of this organization. After all, VCs buy companies to sell them. Could James convince prospective buyers of the company's worth if he couldn't even get his team to fully believe in him?

James first had to identify the man he really wanted to be, the man he longed to believe he is, by considering the qualities he most respected and responded to in himself. In doing this, he was able to both set aside his fear-based coping mechanisms (both the "buddy-buddy" and know-it-all habits), and focus on being the leader and mentor his company needed him to be. Once he named this Radical Success image shift, he had to identify both process goals and outcome goals to get there. Without a doubt, he knew his outcome goal was greater self-respect. When he looked at where his self-respect was lacking, he could identify gaps in his relationship to three primary aspects of himself: social insecurities, his physical presence, and his thoughts.

VISION QUEST

Throughout your day, as you walk into each engagement, notice how you think of yourself. Is your impression of yourself a positive one? Whatever you engage in, practice choosing a very positive image of yourself in relation to whatever is happening. Notice how it feels to actively select a supportive self-image.

His process goals with respect to his physical presence were about getting fit. He'd have to start exercising, and eating for fuel rather than for pleasure. He'd also need to get over his reluctance to spend money on himself, and invest in a wardrobe commensurate with the role he wanted to play. With regard to shifting his relationship with his team, his process goal was not only to increase his instances of one-on-one time with direct reports and colleagues, but also to cultivate an awareness practice, to help him resist the fear-based thoughts urging him to fill every conversation with his own voice. His rush to fill every second of silence was a major handicap in his dignity and his leadership. By creating a practice of clearing his mind before he engaged with any issue, he was able to increase the extent to which he allowed others to do the talking, and to be right. This meant being present enough to hear their problems and working through questions with them to create great solutions *together*. More patience, less politics.

For James, measurement of his progress meant recording the frequency and duration of those one-on-one conversations, tracking his personal self-care, identifying and noting how much he listened, how much he allowed himself to be the student. But it also meant noting how he felt in relation to his idea of himself as *steady, strong, and respected* as a result of each of these choices.

CONSTANT CHANGE

Begin to view the world looking for evidence of evolution. As you engage with others or simply observe yourself, notice each way in which you are able to divert from your habituated responses. How does that feel?

To filter and curate the messages he absorbed, James followed the rest of the process. He put himself on a steady diet of biographies of great humans who inspired him, and sought out the friendship of another senior executive at a leading company in his area, someone he greatly admired. Fueled by competition, he wrote down daily wagers with himself around just what he could accomplish with respect to each of his goals, and he commented on each at the end of the day. That his boss displayed many of the qualities James respected was an immediate and fortunate source of inspiration. His wife and family had a common reaction, though, responding with mixed feelings to change. Their support for his physical health practices was seemingly 100 percent – that is, until it meant early morning wake-ups on the weekends to make time for running, or requesting salads for himself when everyone else was chowing down at a barbecue. Like any human, James felt pressured by their judgment and fear, and by his own fear of losing their love. Stepping outside of those immediate fears, he began to see with compassion and a gentle heart how terrified they were of this strange man who no longer nursed himself to sleep each night with a whisky in one hand and cradling the remote control in the other.

No matter how much of a no-brainer James' process toward his CEO goal may seem, none of the shifts he made involved his politicking for the promotion. All of them had to do with James *aligning* with what he longed to believe was true of himself: that he was a leader worthy of respect and empowerment at the highest level. As you consider your own longed-for truths, you may notice that your particular "intention keepers" or "factors of success" vary from James' choices. They should. Each factor requires you to take ownership of your change process by personalizing it, crafting your own strategy for staying true to your goals.

In working this process through with thousands of professionals, I have been amazed to witness how people very naturally respond positively to certain of these ten factors of success, and just as automatically reject others. Be willing to be surprised. No matter your first reaction to each of them, they are all available as resources. By carefully considering even the ones that might not have initially appealed to you, you may find added power that helps you to stay the course. The factor you valued least at first may actually be the one that makes a difference in a moment where you might otherwise have given up.

Alignment Assignment

1. Acknowledge your ability to make change in your life. Consider your life in ten-year increments—what are instances of before-and-after that you can recall having implemented?

2. Considering these changes, what factors of success do you feel helped you stay your course?

3. What are changes you have seen in the lives of others around you? How is life forcing others around you to adapt and change? What changes do people institute voluntarily? Which type of change is more inspiring to you?

4. Acknowledge your first-blush reactions to each factor. Which might be a change-maker that helps you achieve a breakthrough? Which of them seems like it would be the most difficult to adopt?

5. Which feels the least relevant to your change initiative? Is that an honest response or fear-based backpedalling?

Chapter 3

HOW DO I BEGIN?

Jeff is a great guy. Married, in his late thirties, he has three kids, and a two-hour commute each way to work on top of a ten-hour day there. At the start of this process, Jeff was the sole household breadwinner, weighing in at 460 pounds of living human flesh. Limited quality of life, persistent fatigue and irritability at work, and an early death seemed a foregone conclusion, and he knew it. The first time we sat down together, his response was along the lines of, "Change? Easy for you to say. Look at my life! How can I possibly make better choices?"

He spent the five weeks following that conversation convinced of his inability to change his life. He looked for and catalogued every shred of evidence to support his conviction. And, like most of us, he was a pretty good detective. Aren't we all experts at finding plenty of justification for the case against change?

In his second coaching session, he spent a full twenty-five of his allotted thirty minutes arguing why having a better life wasn't possible for him. The brick wall he had built between who he felt himself to be and any possibility of being different was so tangible, it was all but visible. Following my instincts, I asked him: "Are you really so in love with being this defeated fat guy? Every statement you make sounds as if you're fighting to keep him. Can you imagine if you fought this hard to *not* be him?"

Something shifted for Jeff when I said this. After a long silence, he heaved himself back in the chair, looked at me, and then closed his eyes and chuckled. He got it! By noticing how desperately he was clinging to the self he had created, he saw that all his stuck-ness was an illusion he had been exerting huge energy to maintain, energy he could redirect in support of a better way of living. With five minutes left in the conversation and the rest of his life to put his wisdom into action, he now had a chance at optimizing.

What life are you supporting? What existence are you fighting to keep? Is it in alignment with the existence you *want*? In the case of Jeff, the core issue wasn't that his weight posed a health threat. That was the symptom. The issue was that he had given up any notion of thriving in favor of his illusion of being a prisoner of his own life. Let's be straight here: Whatever you are experiencing in life, you are supporting it, whether you actually like your life or not. And you have a *choice*. Refusing to recognize this freedom to choose is adhering to an illusion that the way you're living is a foregone conclusion—stuck, done, and set in stone. This illusion needs to be jettisoned.

Are you ready to dis-illusion yourself? Say the word "disillusionment," and most people nod their heads in understanding. The way we use the word commonly is to suggest that, like some divine trickster making the cruelest of jokes, life promises certain things and then doesn't come through with them, betraying us, letting us way, way down. It's such a recognizable sentiment: feeling you have things sorted out when *wham*— suddenly something happens to make you realize you're in the middle of a giant failure to understand, connect, get the rules straight, win, or even get in the game. But life itself is incapable of betraying you. Only your illusions have that capacity. By creating illusions and allowing them to function as unconscious convictions about "how things are in the world," you betray life and all its inherent freedoms. Instead of being a negative experience, what if dis-illusionment is an empowering one, a necessary step toward living without self-limiting illusions?

An ironic punchline to this cosmic joke is that assuming you're doomed to be enslaved by your current circum-stances or choices is merely the result of having made those choices many times. The fatalistic setup implied is that life just isn't ever going to give you a break, so why bother even trying to evolve your life to the way you'd like it to be? But if this takeaway were valid, then you'd still be in a crib, or you'd be a caveman lying on a dirt floor.

No matter how you cling to false notions of being stuck or permanently fastened to a single way of being, advances in brain science show that the human mind is infinitely adaptable, and your neuromuscular system is wired to respond to stimuli, both externally and internally generated. While you can't unlearn what you already know, neuroscience confirms that your freedom and power lie fully in your ability to embrace the new, no matter how challenging or scary. The history of the human species is proof-positive of your ability to change.

There is a dangerous idea many people hang onto—that special flaws deprive you of some ultimate state of happiness that most other people can achieve. For some it might take shape as a sustained sense that you'll never be successful in one area or another. For others it might relate to lack of conventional physical beauty, absence of some skill or talent, or personality deficit that lowers your likeability. Illusions of stuck-ness might even have you believing that because some event or experience has happened in your life, you will never be quite who others have a chance to be. Ironically, you may take comfort in smug superiority *because* of this unfortunate event, which leads you to cling to your limitation. Examples of this aren't pretty and usually involve clinging to a sense of victimhood. For example: the heartbreak that convinces you to never love again; the accident or health incident that caused you to allow yourself to fall out of love with life, quit trying, or simply withdraw entirely; the business loss that you let "ruin you for life;" the setback in school that you use to convince yourself to give up. Alternatively, you may find you brandish superiority over others you perceive as being even worse off.

These comparisons just distract you from your fears about your own lot in life and the dreams that lie beyond them. They help you unconsciously choose to be remain stuck, never suspecting that it is a self-fulfilling prophecy. What a wholly avoidable waste.

All of your thoughts influence the microcosm called *you*. From your very first sentient moments in life, you began forming convictions and correlations defined as good/bad, benefit/struggle, suffer/thrive. You compile a dossier on what it means to win and what it means to lose, what you are likely to triumph in and where you're destined to fail. You create every mechanism you can think of to avoid whatever pain you have experienced in the past, thinking the avoidance of such will lead to happiness. It doesn't, though. It just leads to stuck-ness.

Through this pain aversion, an ecosystem is formed, a system of actions and reactions, norms and preferences, all of which you use to keep yourself "safe," not just in the physical sense, but socially and economically, as well. This includes the sorts of education you seek or avoid, the field employment you pursue, your ideas about what constitutes socializing, how you define relaxation, and everything that for each of us becomes the definition of *normal*. You build your life to keep yourself safely nestled in that normal.

Most of us can describe our foundational "normal" for life. When you look at it, you can see that the cycle of rising each day, feeding yourself, somehow interacting with the world, then returning home to rest has a familiarity, a comforting quality. When you take an honest look at "what's happening now," you can see that essentially your life has maintained this basic vibe with some degree of variation, including lamenting the bad days, celebrating the good days, liking some of what you see around you, and disliking the rest. If you really narrow your focus on the whole picture, it's not so tough to ask yourself: How's all that working out? Am I happy? How do I feel as a result of all these unconscious choices? Am I living Optimally or just getting by?

You've made these choices as an expert—each of us is an expert on the person we refer to as "me," the person you've built yourself to be. Your refined skills led to choices that have resulted in every form of success you've ever experienced, every moment of comfort and safety. As such, you have to respect them, but *they can only take you so far*. Your expertise is more specific to the person you've built yourself into than the person you *truly are* or are *capable of becoming*. If you can see your version of life clearly enough to recognize it as the result of your choices so far, you're only a heartbeat away from asking if that's all there is. Aside from what you already have experienced in this lifetime, *what else* is possible for you? A key to Radical Success is becoming an expert in that.

False convictions of being better or worse than others, uniquely blessed or damned, or skilled in "A" but sucky at "B," really don't do you any good at all. These illusions about your existence become firmly held beliefs that limit how much you're willing to gamble on life. Imagine having no preconceived notions of what it means to "be"—instead embodying a blank slate ready to be written upon. Ever wish you could erase all your self-limiting thoughts or negative narratives? Can you imagine how freeing it would feel to be whatever it is you want to be? Rock star. Quarterback. Martin Scorsese. Eleanor Roosevelt. Steve Jobs. Patti Smith. Ray Charles. Coco Chanel. This absence of defining limitations is exactly the dis-illusionment you're going for – living without limiting illusions. Dis-illusionment is your best friend.

At some point, the illusion that your life is permanently, unchangeably as it is became your foregone conclusion. In the case of Jeff, he had decided the choices he was making were the *only* choices possible, ergo the Jeff he experienced *to his way of thinking* was the only Jeff he could be. As someone standing outside of his illusions, you can easily see them as false convictions that don't serve him. But you each have your own set of false convictions that you need to let go of. This is exactly the illusion that you have to "dis" in your own life.

FLEX & FLEXIBILITY

As with beginning any new endeavor, you have to integrate a concept and reinforce it with action. Each morning, as you preview your day, decide one thing you are going to change. It could be as simple as the order in which you conduct your day, some habit of dressing, a food selection. The point is to break with your normal. Notice your level of comfort in doing so – whether comfortable or not, you gain insight regarding your resistance to or acceptance of change. Throughout the week, try to up your ante – choose increasingly significant habits to challenge.

You might be conscious of some of your false convictions, but many of them are so entwined with your modus operandi, your primordial sense of how to survive from one moment to the next, that to ask whether you are aware of this mental scaffolding is a bit like asking whether a fish is aware of water. The fish only knows to move its gills, look for food, and to avoid sucking on sharp objects. What do you know? What are your assumed life fundamentals? If you were to identify and take ownership of all that you consider to be *you*, what would those things be? If you were to outline this living system that is *you*, what would that outline look like?

This is the first step toward making a real change: identifying the unique ecosystem you've chosen by creating it. In looking at this, you can begin to separate who you really are from the parameters and habits you've installed in your life. By seeing your self-selected guardrails as choices, you step into the possibility of making new, better choices.

PERSPECTIVE DIRECTIVE

We all do it from time to time—we embrace our long-standing perspectives and values with an almost religious fervency. This bolsters a false identity, and often becomes an excuse to judge others. When you find yourself experiencing a contrasting value set or perspective on any given topic, rather than judging that person, experiment with trying on their opposing viewpoint. Why might that person feel the way they do? How does that viewpoint expand or contract their experience of the world or the number of options they experience? What does this tell you about your own sacred truths or "holy cows?"

So let's say there's a giant arrow pointing at this moment in time, a sort of multidimensional *You Are Here*. How would you describe *here*? It's easy enough to do that physically (in my chair, at work, on the train, in bed), but can you do it evolutionarily? Can you describe exactly what is going on in your life, what your rhythms and habits are, what fills your time and occupies your thoughts, how you feel physically and mentally, what you like about who you are, and what you are ready to do without? Pull out a sheet of paper and try it.

I Am Here:	What my life is like, what I do, what I don't do, what is normal during the week, during a weekend, who I hang out with, how I usually spend my free time, what is my energy level, etc.
Basic Life Description	
What do I want to keep or have more of?	

What do I want to eliminate?	
What do I wish I had in my life?	
Summarizing NOW:	

Presence and honesty with *yourself* are key to this endeavor. Committing your thoughts to paper heightens your ability to really listen to yourself. By writing, you are forced to confront the question of what the truth really is. It's a process of considering, choosing, writing, and reading of what you just wrote, all of which can help you catch yourself when you're glossing over the facts or being less than truthful. Be sure not to rationalize or talk yourself out of any instinctive reactions to these questions. If you hate something, even if it's not rational or acceptable to certain people in your life for you to say you wish you could eliminate it, go ahead and say so. This description uncovers the game you are playing, your strategy for winning and achieving in your own version of relative success.

An important step towards Game-Changing your life is clearly identifying whatever your old image stands for, what it means and feels like to be as you are. Put simply, what are the adjectives or phrases that sum up how you've been living? There will always be good mixed in with the aspects you'd like to change— so you have to be careful to acknowledge and give proper respect to the things you really like about your life. You're not going to throw the baby out with the bathwater—this process isn't another checklist, a collection of things you have to do in order to have a perfect life in the opinion of some magazine, religious figure, or well-meaning parent. It's living by design— and you're the designer. So take a look at that old house you've been living in. After you've taken yourself on a tour of all its features, the good, the bad, the unsightly, nail it down to a few words: What do you see?

Alignment Assignment

1. What adjectives do you use to describe your life? Which words sum up what you like about it? What words sum up what you don't like about it?

2. What limiting rules have you made for and about yourself? (I always...I only...I can't ever...I have to...I am so...) What are the limiting rules you believe about the world? Leave as few stones

unturned as you possibly can. Ask yourself how you feel about social class, race, work, love, sex, food, fun, sports, sweat, children, God, no God, nature, comfort, etc.

3. What convictions do you observe others around you maintaining? How do those convictions influence their lives? What are the trade-offs? What fears may underlie those convictions?

4. Notice your routines: What things do you do as if on autopilot, unquestioningly? What states of energy do you experience as you move through your day? What are the fluctuations?

Part 2
IN PLAY

Chapter 4

HOW MUCH FREEDOM AND POWER DO I HAVE IN CREATING MY LIFE?

Here are two conflicting notions most of us harbor: We very much want to have the power to create the life we want, but simultaneously believe we don't have that power. Do you, in fact, have that power? It depends. How free do you believe you are? You are only as powerful as you are free—and in case you ever doubt it, let me remind you: You are absolutely free.

To unleash the power of your own true longing, you must acknowledge your essential freedom. Since reading the last chapter, you've been observing the constructs of your life with as much neutral scrutiny as you can muster, honoring the goal of identifying what you like and what you don't, and considering what serves you and what sabotages your happiness. How does the picture look?

Once you awaken to seeing the framework you have built for what it really is, there's no putting yourself back to sleep. You can't pretend it's anything other than a construct of your own making, no matter how inconvenient that knowledge may be for your cozy old ecosystem. And if you're really going for Game-Changing and Radical

Success, there's a chance it will be disastrously inconvenient. This chapter is all about mustering the energy to buck your own system, and access the power you've had all along.

One client of mine, Lorena, took a good look and bucked her system to change her game. At the time I worked with her, she was a single, forty-something Chief Marketing Officer of a successful national retail chain. A self-described lover of professional challenge, she had settled into a nasty situation at work. Whereas she had once enjoyed a relative love-fest in her interactions with others in the organization, now, increasingly, her colleagues were hesitant to work with her. And she was growing distrustful of them as well. Her interactions had gotten so bad, both within her team and across the other departments, that, to her horror, the CEO put her on performance review. Having routinely forfeited any semblance of a personal life for fourteen-hour days in her quest to be the perfect professional, she now felt angry and betrayed. Absolutely bankrupted by her choices, Lorena found no shortage of easy targets for complaint. Operations was wrong for being operational, Sales for being sales-oriented, the economy for being the economy, her own team for burning out, and the CEO for being a good CEO and forcing her to address the situation. Like blaming the rain for being wet, these actions left her with nothing at the end of the day but her own unhappiness.

The real problem? Her "normal" just didn't work. Her convictions about herself and her resulting actions created a self-sabotaging ecosystem in which she could not flourish, one she mistook for unquestionable reality. Once she recognized that she was deeply invested in her story of being a passionate workaholic, and that she had woven all her life experiences into a trusty support for her conviction that this is *who she is* and that's just *how life is*, the insights began appearing. In looking carefully at the many ways she had been betraying herself each day in order to live up to an idea that left her energetically bankrupt, it became clear that she had created a set of assumptions, norms, and actions that in no way supported her in her efforts to become her definition of Optimal. While she held the illusion that she was a passionate professional, in truth she was a self-betraying martyr looking for accolades and veneration from others. No wonder she had become one pissed-off CMO (Chief Martyrdom Officer). No wonder no one wanted to work with her. The game she was playing? Brilliant suffering saint who ends up alone and unappreciated. For someone suffering to that degree, the money is no consolation. Win or lose, it's an awful game to play.

WHAT GAME ARE YOU PLAYING?
TAKING A CLOSER LOOK.

Are you beginning to recognize that there's a lot you're doing that is not Optimal, and doesn't *truly serve* you? Welcome to reality. When you begin to honestly examine your life, like many people, you might find the picture doesn't look or feel very good. Whether there's an outcome you always thought you would have nailed by now, or there's a higher level of peace or happiness you want, careful inventory of the quality and substance of your days will make it transparently obvious that your state of disappointment results directly from your daily choices. You need a course correction, *stat*.

So, what if you acted on your own freedom to choose and eliminated everything that does not truly serve you, never to experience those things ever again? What would life look like then? Likely it would mean recapturing a whole lot of energy. It would feel a lot more Optimal.

First, let's be clear about the phrase "truly serve." When you ask yourself if something is truly in service of your highest good, you have to bear in mind what it brings about in your life, both concretely and experientially. With any action, whether it's taking part in a routine social commitment or eating a particular food without thinking, ask yourself: Does this serve me? Something can serve you in lots of ways, and that's the tricky part. For example, a social commitment may make you feel less lonely or as if you are part of a community, but if the experience is not in itself satisfying or somehow otherwise conflicts with what you want for yourself (maybe a good night's sleep, some time alone, etc.), then, in honesty, it absolutely does not serve or work in support of your Radical Success. A food might make you happy because of how it tastes on your tongue, but if it's making you unhealthy, it's definitely not serving you. Cigarettes might give you a moment of escape and a nicotine rush, but they don't work in service of your well-being. Zoning out on social media or some TV show may shift you out of work-think, but does it serve your quality of life? In the case of Lorena, hanging her identity on being the Chief Martyrdom Officer definitely didn't serve *anyone*, least of all herself.

We all know change is tough. The culture that is your life is shaped by how you think, process, and behave in relationship to your external world. It has been adapted to keep you safe *as you are now*. When you begin to tweak little behaviors here and there, you act on your freedom. You introduce change/discomfort into an ecosystem that, on the surface, appeared to be in equilibrium. Usually, unless you get scared into taking the initiative through a personal disaster, such as a health crisis, job loss, some sort of strong interpersonal conflict or other disruption, your attempts to voluntarily address an issue within the ecosystem are not likely to take hold. Even then, without a Game-Change, you're likely to play the same game all over again, however the dynamics unfold. There's just not enough to motivate you. So how do you make a lasting shift towards what is radically true for who *you* are?

It helps to put your eye on the prize. What is it that you really want for yourself? Before you confront the difficult step of abandoning those comfy, cozy, unconscious actions and beliefs that result in a life you *don't* want, get yourself excited and juiced up with visions of what you *do* want. It will be a lot less scary to act on your freedom by challenging your norms if you support that effort with a strong sense of what the reward will be for doing so. If you're going to rip away the rose-colored glasses, make sure there's something even sweeter in sight. Get real about what you *yearn* for. Get really hungry for the payoff. Longing is the ultimate ally.

Even if your entire life has been built on wanting to please and win approval from others, when you ask that heart of yours what it most dearly wants out of life, it won't know how to lie. Invoking the power of your own personal truth, when you ask yourself how you want to feel every day, what you want your attitude to be, what you want your level of energy to be, and how you want to encounter whatever comes your way, you step out of false victimhood and transform the refrain of "Life is beyond my control" into "How I live is utterly within my control." That's a really great place to be. Repeat each of those statements to yourself. Which one leaves you feeling better?

Lorena had to start by acknowledging that her unconscious convictions so far hadn't provided any hope of being happy, and probably wouldn't ever. In retrospect, she said: "It was like looking for my mortal enemy and finding her in the mirror." Unsteady at first, she allowed herself to explore this vast expanse of absolute freedom in choosing. She realized that most, if not all, of her choices had been made to support a life that had nothing to do with allowing her to thrive. They in no way correlated to being the masterful leader of her own life she aspired to be, much less the leader of others. They gave her nothing. Zero. Zip. Supporting her workaholic identity was driven 100 percent by *what she wanted others to think of her*. She wasn't happy, but she had successfully achieved workaholism. Others clearly felt unnerved and powerless in the face of the rage that surfaced from her frustration and exhaustion. Keeping this up consumed so much attention and energy that Lorena had none left to give to the pursuit of being *truly alive*.

Owning her inadvertent enmity of herself unleashed the freedom to consider what being fully alive might mean to her. By identifying and admitting to what she most deeply longed for, a whole new Lorena began to emerge. This version of Lorena not only made time for what made her feel alive, she *insisted* upon it with the same exacting attitude she had previously reserved for her enslaved relationship with work. She prioritized the experience of exercising her body several times a week. She returned to previously neglected interests, such as drawing and horseback riding. Fueled by freedom and the peace that comes from taking empowered action, Lorena's nervous system could relax. She was more creative. The people who reported to her no longer had to endlessly try to compensate for her unhappiness. As her relationship with herself became trusting and friendly, issues at the office were able to be resolved through reasonable negotiations rather than battles. No longer did each issue mark a milestone in gaining personal power. Lorena was far from falling off her professional pedestal. In fact, her performance improved drastically as she became more efficient and adopted an approach of collaboration rather than a "last man standing" competition.

Dig deep and be brutally honest about how you really want to live. In complete freedom, there is no shying away or backpedaling, and no room for apologies or excuses. There is only one question that matters: *How do you want to feel in this lifetime?* If you think this is silly, I suggest you consider the absurd silliness of living an entire lifetime feeling frustrated and limited.

ABANDON LOGIC, ALL YE WHO GAME-CHANGE HERE

When you're engaging in this type of Optimal life envisioning, remember one thing: This is no time for logic. Longing is not about logic. It's about what you want to create with your freedom during your next 34 million moments on this planet. It's about how you want to *feel* about why you're here.

As you contemplate your truest longings, whatever comes up is valid. If you're 4' 8" tall and always have dreamt of being Magic Johnson, I encourage you to write down exactly how playing basketball professionally would have made you feel, and why that would have been great. If you're tone deaf and wish you had been a lead singer in a rock band, write what you think that would have felt like, and what you would have loved about it. Think of this exercise as excavating your heart for clues and insights about your truest sense of "happy."

What You Long For	Payoffs

Whether you come up with a single phrase or feel a
lot of words bubbling up to the surface, jot them down.
You can note them here on this page, on the back of a
receipt in your wallet, in pixel form—it doesn't matter
where, just commit them to writing. This is the navigational true north that you'll use to make decisions moving
forward. Once the flow of words slows or stops, look at
what you've written and ask, what else? What else do I
really want to be my default experience in this lifetime?
Then keep writing. If something comes up that you push
away, thinking it is "out of character" or somehow just
not within your reach, write it down anyhow. If negative
judgments, critiques, or objections come up, write them
down only so you can recognize how you have systemati-
cally rejected your own freedom. Until now, that is.

NARRATIVE IMPERATIVE

Practice listening to the story you tell yourself, and others, about
your self. Do you put yourself down? Do you use phrases such as
"I would have, but...." When you listen attentively to your underlying set of convictions, what do you hear? What have you come
to believe is true about yourself? Among those narratives, identify
the ones that are most supportive of your idea of Radical Success,
and avoid repeating the ones that are not.

When you've gone at this for five minutes, take a look at
what you have written down. Can you summarize, epitomize
or motto-ize your longing into a statement? A phrase?

When working with folks to define how they really
want to feel in relation to life, many strong phrases have
come up: "In my zone" or "Top form" or "Enlightened

self-interest" or "On my A game." For my own life, I've used the term "rock star" to describe the energy I want to feel, not in terms of sex, drugs, and a Stratocaster, but rather in terms of authentic self-expression, freedom, courage, presence, and sexiness. One woman called it "Sizzling strength". One guy said "One hundred percent." No matter what your catch phrase is, it should feel epic. That's right, *epic*.

EXCITE & INSIGHT

What excites you? Who on the planet turns you on? By paying attention to what you look up to or cherish, you get valuable insight into what you really feel excitement about. If no one comes to mind, go to a bookstore or hop online and ask yourself *who (italics...or whom)* you would like to know more about. Research those people with scientific scrutiny, not only for their accomplishments, but for any struggles they may have overcome and any practices they credit with speeding them towards victory. How can you apply their evolutionary story to your own?

You will know if you've really been true to your longing by this test: When you look at that list, it should excite you. It should literally make you feel pumped up, juicy, and just a little incredulous. Your own longing should turn you on. Who you really are should make you feel hot. The notion of feeling that way every day should be so tantalizing that it makes your mouth water a little and your heart smile a lot. You'll know you've nailed your starting point if it makes you chuckle to yourself, or glance over your shoulder to make sure the guy in seat 2B isn't peeking over your keyboard to see what you just wrote.

Just as your heart doesn't know how to lie, your body doesn't, either. When you like something, it is visceral. In the same way that ideas and people and places that you like make you feel good, the life you're creating should make you feel good inside your skin, all the way down into your gut. Acknowledging within yourself that there are a whole lot of possibilities you've never explored causes you to release serotonin, dopamine, and all sorts of problem-solving, happy-feeling chemicals, biological human creativity juice that literally tells your body: "We've got some good moments coming—things are about to get better!"

So why don't we just go toward those things that make our brains release happy chemicals? Because there's also a part of us that suppresses this. This mechanism is a holdover from ancient survival concerns. To keep you "safe" within your established normal, your brain will sometimes interject with historic convictions (however false they may be) to try to get you to like people, activities, or things you don't actually like, just for the sake of whatever social safety they might provide. This can take the expression of marrying the person who might be "good on paper," hanging out with the crowd you don't relate to, taking the job that nauseated you even during the interviewing process, etc. Often you do these things based on some sense of material gain or financial security, but usually what you're really motivated by is safety and social standing. Don't think you need to be ashamed of ever having made any of these choices. We all have. Game-Change is about recognizing those choices as opportunities to evolve beyond whatever drove them. It's about learning from how they made you feel with respect to your own life. Radical Success means changing this game forever.

That historic voice of conviction also tries to dissuade you from enjoyment, not because it's evil or bent on your misery, but because it's all it knows how to do. Although the U.S. Constitution protects the pursuit of happiness, most of us in the course of growing up are taught more about pursuit of trappings of safety, social standing, and relative success. With that conditioning, anything outside of that narrow purview can trigger alarms. Enjoyment? Oooh, radical. Alarm signals shut down the production of a collection of chemicals that give you good feelings (loosely referred to as "endorphins") and jump-starting production of the fear-provoking hormone, adrenaline. As a matter of habit, your brain hears, "What do you really want?" and all it can come up with is a habituated refrain: "money, status, car, sex, food, sleep, safety" (not necessarily in that order), all things society has told you are measures of your success. To achieve your desired radically successful state, you have to step outside of that feedback loop and bravely identify your most valued feelings.

Be compassionate with yourself: Realize that it's infinitely more safe to pursue and measure success extrinsically than it is to discard that conditioned modus operandi in favor of cultivating your happiness based on experiences alone. And don't be surprised if somewhere inside your head there's a voice whispering: "Hey wait, if Optimal experience is the measure of success, how the heck do you make sure everyone knows you won?" Trust me, they'll know. They'll know because thanks to your neuro-cognitive patterns never going away, you're not ever going to forget how to achieve the extrinsic stuff anytime you want it. To boot, the more you engage in these things that actually do delight you, others around you will experience in you a dignity and fulfillment that renders all those achievements either even more enjoyable, or not at all worthwhile, in which case you'll discard them like broken luggage. Spending time and energy pursuing them in the hope of achieving happiness is like trying to get the affection and comfort of a pet from a motorcycle. This is why when you start to explore what you really want, you must focus your attention by asking very direct questions about feeling, experience, and sensation. It's this simple:

WHAT DO YOU WANT TO FEEL?

_____

_____

_____

_____

_____

_____

_____

Don't worry if that refrain of money, food, sex, sleep, cars, safety, or some variation along these lines, is what you hear first – of course you do, because for the past however many decades that's all you've been told, or told yourself, that you want. What if wanting those things is a given? What if they are the *duh*, not even worth mentioning? Let's assume you want those things. Then dedicate your list to fundamental, experiential, Radical Success.

Now that you've acknowledged your freedom to name how you really want to feel in life, you're going to start to free up energy to sustain that feeling. That *is* your power to change.

Alignment Assignment

1. Remind yourself of your desired state as often as possible, starting first thing in the morning and as often as possible during every single phase of your day. Identify anchors that can help you to *remind yourself* to remind yourself – your phone ringing, a colleague coming by, top of the hour, etc.

2. Notice experiential highs and lows throughout your day—is there a pattern or correlation you can make between aligning with your desired state or betraying it?

3. What are the highs that result from your own choices? The lows?

4. What are the things you tell yourself you do for a high, but when you observe yourself doing them, you realize they actually result in experiential lows?

5. Are there activities/people/things you resist or shrink from when you think of them, which give you an experiential high when you actually encounter them?

6. Are there any insights or experiences to add to what you've already described as either your old normal (the snapshot of what you're ready to be done with), or to your desired state list?

Chapter Five

HOW WILL I KNOW
WHAT TO DO?

Surrender to your dreams. That's what you have to do. To live them, you must acknowledge them. Let them own you, 100 percent. They know exactly what to do.

Trusting your dreams can be a challenge, because you have been conditioned to distrust and disregard them. It's so much easier to look around externally for what you should work toward next rather than asking for guidance from within. Because of this, you know countless ways to push the wisdom of your dreams and visions aside. One of the most common habits of discontent is playing the game in which you complain about life as if you're powerless to change it. Your dreams have another way of playing, and their only game is for you to play *big*. They only know how to direct you to be absolutely true to them.

If doubts are coming up about your ability to change directions and make choices based on your dreams instead of your old convictions, remind yourself of all the times in the past when life events have forced you to adjust your actions. There are more choices on the menu than you've tried. Every single human being who makes choices different from your own is living proof that you *can* do things differently than you already have been.

I saw a beautiful example of this when I taught Business Creativity & Mastery as part of the Advanced Management program at NYU. One of the students was a senior executive named Newton whose relationship with life had definitely steered him in the direction of a slow turn for the worse. Bright, thoughtful, socially skilled, he had held senior positions at some of the top tech companies on the planet. The esteem he enjoyed from his colleagues and community had earned him a five-star-studded Rolodex, and his ability to generate new ideas and problem-solve made him an automatic go-to in both his professional and personal life. Despite having all this going for him, through a series of professional choices, somehow Newton found himself languishing as an administrator at one of the nation's leading business schools. His passion was waning under the duress of intense internal politics, and despite having the benefit of taking some coaching and leadership development courses, he just wasn't able to put his heart into his work anymore. It was affecting his relationships with staff and family, as his conversation topics were becoming increasingly narrow and negative. Newton was thinking, sounding, and acting a lot more like a bitter victim than an inspiring professional at the top of his game. Further complicating matters, as the single source of financial security for his family in a down economy and slow job market, he felt trapped. If ever there were a candidate for an injection of passion and possibility, Newton was it. He had the perfect conditions for taking his life from "good enough" to radically successful.

When he first engaged in questioning what he truly wanted, his automatic responses were all about what was wrong with the administration he managed, all the ways he wished they would be different from how they were, who the issues were created by, how he thought they should change their ways of behaving, etc. Aside from the obvious, that attempting to change others around you is utterly fruitless, talking to Newton about his goals was about as inspiring as a trip to the dump. If those were his dreams, they were a dead end. They didn't offer any forward moving possibilities or chance for greater fulfillment.

The problem Newton faced was he had abdicated his power to choose what he wanted in life. Rather than focusing upon his desired experiences, he was fixating on what he *didn't* want in life. There's no way to win that game, and sadly, he's not alone. From coaching thousands of adults across many lifestyles, functions, and organizations, I've learned that for many of us, the ability to nurture our dreams has become incredibly elusive. Most of us have forgotten to bother harboring any dream whatsoever, let alone dedicating time and energy to actually nurturing them.

I called Newton's attention to the fact that what he was holding out as a "dream" was nothing more than a sophomoric critique of the people around him, which couldn't therefore be expected to yield any positive outcome, much less the sublime experience of deep fulfillment. He knew it was true. As he shifted his focus from lamenting the human foibles around him to really asking himself what he wanted, slowly an image began to emerge in his mind of working independently, participating in the excitement of the social media world, monetizing both his Rolodex and his ability to build community, and stepping up to act as a thought leader. He didn't know how he was going to make it happen, but by asking his own consciousness what it truly longed for, Newton created and planted the seed of a new identity that he slowly made reality. Fast-forward four years; he now lives comfortably earning a living as head of his own successful social media consultancy.

Distrusting your ability to live your dreams directly correlates to the natural preference for staying "comfortable." You're not going to evolve your life to an Optimal state without getting intentionally uncomfortable. You've got to Game-Change by soldiering through the discomfort by keeping yourself moving in support of your ideas. That's why the new concept of who *you* are is so important: You have to want to be that person so much that *that's* who you begin being, right now. You must become relentless to ensure that your Optimal thrives from the very start.

When you're going on a road trip in real life, you choose your destination and give yourself what you need to get there—a map, a GPS, and directions. When you're plotting your Game-Change, you've got to do the very same things: Name your destination and identify the actions to get there. You don't set out for Heaven and then follow a road map to Hell. At least, not if you actually want to get there.

With the various self-assessments you've been doing so far, you're aggregating a lot of information about yourself. At this point, it can be really helpful to use visual tools to keep your eye on the goal—some people find having a diagram helps keep them focused. As a visual learner myself, I use the following chart to clarify my path. This isn't a perfect representation of this stage of Game-Change, just my way of thinking about it that might help you reflect and solidify your notion of what you're going for. I like imagining that what I'm stepping out of is on the left hand side of my map, and what I'm building toward is on the right hand side. I invite you to use this chart, or make up your own:

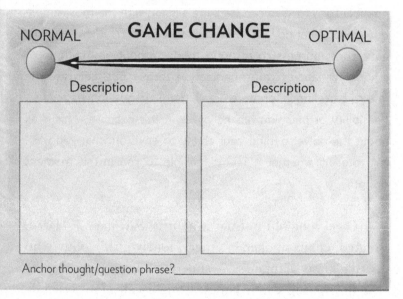

Once you've noted what's the before and what's the projected after, get ready to ride. If you're really going to get on the road, you've got to walk through and then firmly shut the door on the mentality that led to the life you've created until now. You've got to kick to the curb any notion that extrinsic achievement and relative success are enough.

Sound brutal? It may be the most compassionate

thing you ever do for yourself. Imagine the brutality of living half a life, of operating on unconscious assumptions while leaving countless possibilities unexplored. *That* is brutal. And non-sensical. Let's agree not to be either of those things.

DREAM MACHINE

Make time to daydream, even if for only 5 minutes a day. Give yourself the mandate to ask yourself whether what you dream is possible for you. You can start the session with the most simple question: "What do I wish would be true for me?" and then allow your consciousness to respond freely without any critique or editing. Whatever your imagination throws out, cultivate the image, barreling in for more detail, more images, more specifics. Feasibility or planning has no place in this exercise. This is all about the power behind your ability to envision what you want for yourself, whether it seems feasible to you in this moment or not.

Give your old normal a name. "Sad man." "Tired, isolated, chain smoker." "Angry, lonely girl." "Guy who doesn't know happiness." "Energetic wipe out." In the case of aspiring CEO, James, I might call him "Friendly Fraidy Cat." By naming the old normal with transparent reference to that which you no longer accept as being good enough, while also naming the state you want to begin to align with, you are creating a conceptual and energetic anchor, something strong enough to get you through your next fifty Game-Changing choices with your loyalty to your Optimal state intact. This is how you begin to own your dreams.

Because here's the bottom line on getting up off the old normal couch and through the door toward acting on your radical longing: Everything that you see in your life right now that you don't like was created with the mentality of the person you have been up until now. You cannot move into a new state of being by asking that old, tired, and worn-out person to get you there. That person, with that mentality, only knows how to give you the results you've gotten up until now. You have to love him or her for their hard work and resourcefulness. Bless them for doing their very best in all matters, but then forever retire them from navigating the path that lies ahead.

This Optimal idea of *you* is the starting point. Don't be distracted by wistful "someday" ideas and statements that are uttered with a sigh. Those are for fairy tales. You or anyone being made content by extrinsic achievements is a fairy tale. The truth: You want to feel viscerally alive, fulfilled, and aligned in your choices. This process says: Look at how you want to feel and begin to be the person who feels that way *now*. Let that ideal dictate every choice from now on. It's a bit like time travel. Physically, you're staying right here in the present moment, but emotionally, you're embodying your desired future state by changing your game, starting right now. That dream is the navigational true north you start with, and through practice and repetition, your Optimal becomes a firmly established reality. Essentially, you're pulling your desired future state out of *someday* and using it as the decision maker *now*. You're surrendering all decision-making to the dream you want to live, letting that dream call all the shots going forward.

You need this new mentality to be the reference point for how to navigate what's ahead, and not just the big decisions like, "Do I take the offer?" or "Should I act on that investment opportunity?" but even the little ones. The little actions are, after all, most influential on your state of being on a moment-by-moment basis, so they actually are going to have a more frequent, immediate impact upon how you experience life. They also offer you the best opportunities to practice Game-Changing. Practicing on the little day-to-day actions and choices, you train yourself to Game-Change on bigger, seemingly more challenging goals. Aligning even your smallest actions reinforces the likelihood that you'll become your dream. It's like lifting the little five-pound barbells when you go to the gym, so that you can gradually work up to the heavy lifting.

It's this simple: The old normal is going to give you the same old answers. The desired, exciting, radically successful self is going to give you new answers that move you closer to the desired state. Period. Choose who to listen to, who to put in the driver's seat. Would you rather hand over the keys to a motivated racecar driver, or to a tired, bloated, and unhappy drunk who just ate too many chicken wings and really needs to go home, chug some water, and go to bed?

Keep a clear sense of what the desired state is and name it. Looking at the various notes and realizations you've had about both the life you've built till now, and what you really want to feel from this point on, how would you boil down into a few words what you really want your life experience to be? In Newton's case, he had to recognize that for him what mattered most in life wasn't the conditions life served up, but what he wanted to build from his own efforts. On his list of characteristics describing the old him, he had more phrases expressing how misunderstood, undervalued, tired, and trapped he felt than phrases about flourishing or living and working in authentic self-expression. Thinking about what qualities he admired most in others, he created a list of guidepost values including words such as dynamic, measured risk-taking, thoughtful, impactful, vibrant, exciting, ideator, connector. To him, these qualities were prerequisites for any experience of "success" he might accomplish. No matter what he might do in life, through this exercise he identified that in order to be fulfilled, he had to feel as if he embodied those characteristics. In uncovering this radical, profound foundation to his own ability to flourish, Newton had taken hold of the key to his own Radical Success. On the list of traits he felt would be embodied by a great man both professionally and personally, his phrases really came to life: *trusted and respected, well connected, doesn't wait for permission, goes for it, fosters learning and insights, experiments with new ideas, is comfortable in himself, confident, empowering.* Comparing the two, the gap was obvious. His old normal was a black hole of indignation. It was "they won't let me," the battle cry of a pouty baby. In contrast, when he looked at how he wanted to be and summarized the many values he had come up with, his idea of his Optimal self was all about being a *creative catalyst.*

This anchor concept of *creative catalyst* allowed him to save all the energy he had previously been wasting on trying to show everyone how wrong they were (alienating them in the process), and begin to stand his ground as a thought leader, someone incrementally impactful in his areas of interest—which was what he'd wanted all along. *Creative catalyst* wasn't only an expression of the longing Newton had unconsciously felt all along. If you recall my mentioning above how well networked he already was, how socially skilled and sought after, you know that he actually already had the resources to *be* the creative catalyst all along. By shifting his awareness and focusing upon himself as a creative catalyst, he was able to drop his opposition to his current situation, and able to experience being a *creative catalyst* more of the time.

Hopefully you've come up with a name for yourself that really resonates and gets the juices flowing, because starting right now, that Optimal self is going to make all the choices that lead you to Radical Success. Asking that version of yourself, or those aspects of yourself, how to confront the next thirty choices begins to draw that state of being out of a vague "someday" or "imaginary future" and invoke it solidly in the here and now. As Albert Einstein said, "We cannot solve our problems with the same thinking we used when we created them."

When you hold your goals in a far-flung, distant future, you avoid being responsible to them right now, and you prevent yourself from taking action in support of them. Defining a goal as a future "maybe" or "someday" indefinitely postpones it. It keeps it from being a present reality, or a real-time up-to-me-and-only-me responsibility. Unless you align with your goals immediately, they stay at a remove, and the possibility of feeling a payoff from them remains remote. When you start to act from the assumption that you already have the states of being necessary to achieve those goals within you, that you just need to activate them and empower them to help you make your choices for yourself, you begin to embody them. Not someday, not after you've lost ten pounds, not after you've gotten permission to write by being guaranteed of making *The New York Times Bestseller List*. You begin to *be* them right n*ow*.

DREAM PERCEIVER

How much of a role does vision play in your conversations with others? In the media? Visions can give expression to desired outcomes, neutral speculation, or situations to be feared or avoided. When you listen to expressions of vision around you, and those made by you, what is the content? Do your expressions of vision focus upon what you want? Do others? How do you respond energetically or internally to these conversations?

When Newton allowed himself to own his dream to be in charge, he moved away from squeaky wheel into confident presence. He experienced people from a perspective of quiet observation, reinforcing his own dynamic, learning nature. He shifted his awareness—instead of looking for any opportunity to show off how amazing but underappreciated he was, he began to pay attention to each person and each situation around him, and to respond effectively to whatever he realized was required in the moment. By letting his dream call the shots, he went from stuck to evolving, and over time evolved himself into a zeitgeist leader in his field.

Chances are, no matter what time of day it is or where you are as you read this, there are some immediate choices on the horizon: to get some good sleep or to text furiously in response to a late night call? To eat a healthy meal or to have another cocktail? To answer the phone on the first ring or to take a few breaths and answer it calmly? To have all the answers or to encourage others to find their own? What if every choice you make for the next week is made with the awareness of how well you Game-Change in support of your Optimal state?

Welcome to your journey. Now get in gear, and go!

Alignment Assignment

1. Observe others actively as you move through your daily life. Watch for indicators of what their attention is usually focused upon. Do you see dreams at work? Do you see fixation on what they don't want or don't like?

2. Can you see alignment or conflict between the values they express and their actions? Are they actively managing themselves to achieve the states of being they reference wanting?

3. Notice people who embody a state similar to what you have identified as your Optimal self. Do their observable values and actions align? What would you say you experience when you are around them? Do you like being in their presence?

4. Notice people who embody a state you are not interested in experiencing, either because you've already been there or you have no interest in going. How do their thoughts, words, and actions align with maintaining that state?

Chapter 6

WHAT ACTIONS WILL MAKE MY DREAMS A REALITY?

Radical Success becomes reality through the Game-Change of aligned action. It begins as an idea of fulfillment, but it comes alive through action.

If you have followed the process in the previous chapters, you've likely designed something you'd like to experience as reality, and although you might be at least a bit incredulous that it could ever actually exist, hopefully you're determined to give it a try. It's your dream, your radically successful self, your version of *as good as it can possibly get.*

Sometimes, though, we've had these dreams buried so deeply inside us for so long that we're afraid to let them come to the surface, because they're reminders of everything we fear we're not.

This was the case with Melanie, a Senior Operations Executive at a well-respected financial services organization. Married and in her mid-thirties, she and her husband hailed from a small town in Iowa. They had earned advanced degrees that made them eligible for lucrative positions in their fields, all with the goal of moving to a major city, a goal they easily achieved. At the time I worked with Melanie, she and her husband were living in San Francisco, and had fallen in love with the variety of food, culture, nightlife, and events that made it easy to meet and hang out with other smart, self-made professionals. The problem was that the level of priority they placed on their career and financial achievements, and on hob-nobbing with other high achievers, left Melanie feeling unfulfilled. She was bloated and too frequently hungover from all the socializing over cocktails. She felt dull in her marriage. She became snippy with colleagues and subordinates at work. She felt at odds with her routine ten to twelve hour days. Although her glamorous lifestyle was making her miserable—and miserable to be around—Melanie was reluctant to change her lifestyle, or even just shift her lifestyle preferences. She thought her success and happiness were contingent upon climbing the career and social ladders.

I wasn't so convinced. Plenty of people enjoy the best of food and culture and even cocktail hour without losing themselves in the process. When I asked Melanie to look carefully at her beliefs about herself, the assumptions she had always harbored about what it meant to *be Melanie*, something happened. She realized that at some point in her youth, she had divided the world into two categories: smart people and physical people. Melanie didn't feel as if she could compete with the jocks in her world, so she constructed her image and identity to what she saw as opposed to theirs—that of a brainiac. Fast-forward a few decades and the highly intelligent small-town teenager who only sees two choices had become a mid-life urban woman lacking even the slightest relationship with her physical self.

Although her professional success provided obvious proof of her acumen, she wasn't using any of her intelligence to support living well. Her habit of wearing shapeless clothing was not born out of style preference, but to literally hide her physical body from others. The rules her teenage self had established long before meant she was oblivious to which kinds of eating habits would best support her and provide energy at work. She thought munching bagged snacks in front of her computer was an antidote to her lack of energy in the earlier part of the day, followed by an espresso chaser or two in the mid-afternoon. At twilight she would dash to meet her husband at the hottest new restaurant for multicourse meals, and later partake in a precious few hours of drunken, unpredictable sleep, only to awaken and repeat the cycle all over again the next morning. Forget about the self-esteem generated by movement, the sexiness of loving one's own body, or the creativity, circadian, and immune functions that result from maintaining a strong connection to the physical self. Like many of us, she had set up a narrow identity, as determined many years before, with all the wisdom and limited resources of her well-meaning preteen self. When you go through life judging every possibility as either *me* or *not me*, your options can become pretty limited. It's the kind of game only optimizing can get us out of.

Your true dreams might include things other people are doing or having, but that nasty inner voice of safety, of old normal, interjects: "Sure, that's fine for *them*, they have _____, _____, and _____," discrediting both their achievements and your ability to do or have the same. Remember that stuck-ness you explored in Chapter Three? Denying someone his or her achievements is a strategy to protect *you* from the pressure of your own desired achievements. Say you're watching someone have something you'd like to have, or be how you would like to be. The courage it takes to say, "I can be that, or have that, and I'm starting right now," is miles away from discrediting your own possibility by saying, "Oh, it's easy for them." In a moment when you might otherwise deny that person their struggle, you have to be generous and credit just how much courage, love, and discipline *they* are mustering to live as they do. Rather than resigning hope, remember *you* have that capacity within you as well.

"Be kind, for everyone you meet is fighting a great battle." It's a quote attributed to numerous thinkers. The first time I encountered those words, I interpreted them as referring to forgiveness—I believed they were essentially a reminder to be kind to people who treat us badly or behave poorly. After doing my own Game-Changing and helping others with it, I realize the phrase offers wisdom about never denying anyone their humanity, their perfectly delivered opportunities to struggle against their own fears, whether they are winning in the face of those fears or not. This phrase and Game-Change itself are all about respect for each person's struggles, all of your strengths, and the ubiquitous capacity for each of us to muster strength beyond what we might have previously imagined possible.

That "old normal" voice can be counted on to surface and insistently deny both your own progress and your ability to overcome. It has to be fought against with everything you've got. Once you begin to hear it, your most powerful tool in subverting it is *action*. When you take action, the resulting experience—most likely a positive one—is the proof positive that the voice is wrong. Game-Changing is really the result of identifying three things: how you want to feel, the thoughts that will support that feeling, and the actions that will make you think and feel that way. This is success as defined not only by me, but by the Game-Changing radical, Mahatma Gandhi. Here's how it unfolds: You identify a feeling you want to experience; you guide your thoughts in toward that experience; then you take action to realize the feeling. Once you've conceived a new idea of what you want to have, or do, or be, it takes aligned actions—actions that make you feel the way you want that idea to make you feel—in order to make that idea real. *Right now.*

AND . . . ACTIONS

I can't stress this enough: Once you figure out exactly how you want to build your life, you have to turn concepts into actions to make them real. In the past chapter you began practicing observing what it looks like to align actions with ideals. You've now observed others either living in support of, or betraying, their truth, and hopefully you've done so with kindness in your heart. You might have gone beyond seeing it with your eyes, and started to feel it in your gut. My experience working with thousands of people as they've gone through this process has shown me that once you view the world with an awareness of people's degrees of alignment with themselves, the tradeoffs become obvious. What people are actually gaining or losing when they do or don't align becomes crystal clear: They are either brimming with natural energy and deep self-confidence, gained through the affirmation of living as they truly desire; or they come across as beaten down and anxious, frantic for validation as they forfeit their dreams and ideals in exchange for familiar, established patterns they and others around them are already conditioned to expect—which ultimately leads only toward relative success. It's that simple.

Martha Stewart gave a great example of this during a live interview at New York City's Beacon Theatre just following her emancipation from house arrest for insider trading. She was in conversation with the editor of *BusinessWeek*, before an audience of journalists eager to witness her reaction to reentry into the public eye. Would she shrink or shine?

Against the stark, unadorned black stage, unfettered by this rapacious crowd, she graced us with her customary self-confidence, fully grounded and without a shred of shame. During the conversation, once her legal woes had been thoroughly dissected, the editor asked Stewart a general question about her life: To what did she attribute her remarkable accomplishments? Without missing a beat, she quickly credited all she had done in her lifetime to being a visionary.

While you can guess that I love that she trumpets the importance of vision, I don't agree that she owes her success to her vision alone. Vision is an important precursor to any empowered action. We all have visions. My dog has visions/dreams when she sleeps. But how many of your thoughts/ideas/visions concern your ambitions and longings, what you wish to experience in life? How many of your thoughts are actually worries, flights of fear-riddled fantasies, or what you *don't* want to happen? From what is conveyed in the press about her disciplined lifestyle, business-minded decisiveness, and exacting standards in output, Martha is a great example of someone who cultivated a vision for her Radical Success early on, and has continued to do so. More importantly, though, she has mustered the discipline to *focus* on her visions, and has made them real through the continual alignment of her actions. Love her or lump her, Martha is a visionary, yes. More importantly, she is an *actionary*—she uses her intention and focus to identify the actions she must take to become an uncommonly accomplished human being. Radical Success lies in actively choosing optimized visions, and then Game-Changing by undertaking aligned actions to bring them to fruition.

If you can, think back on an instance or two in which, given an array of compelling choices and in the interest of bringing about a desired outcome, you or someone around you noticeably aligned an action that contradicted an old habit. Let that ground you while you consider the following: *What will you do to thrive in the way you dream of thriving?* Hopefully, embracing your dream has already revealed some surprises, ideas that the old you would never have given you permission to think about, much less act upon. So let's keep the thrive alive, and identify actions that will help you make your dreams reality.

To make the new *you* happen, you have to begin to make him/her real. When you look at your list of who or how you want to be, what energy you want to feel, how you want to think, etc., you've got a navigational true north for every next step you take. Now, having observed it passively, you're going to start to fill in what your Game-Changing self does proactively.

Look at your dream. Maybe you see in it qualities or states of being you want to aspire to. Maybe you've already identified some actions as being necessary aspects of living as the person you want to be. With your idea as your starting point, you have the blueprint for what that way of living will look and feel like—now let's put flesh on the bones.

For any quality or state of being you have identified, ask what actions or activities produce that feeling. Write down as many verbs as you can possibly think of that lead to the desired states of being. Don't let the voice of doubt or judgment slow down the flow. When the critical voice tries to prevent you from jotting something down, perhaps write it *twice* for an extra nudge forward. Any interference from that voice you were long ago taught to call "the voice of reason" is simply not welcome here.

If, as you conjure actions or experiences that secretly delight you, the historic convictions start getting ugly, bust them up by taunting them a little. I like to tease mine with "Oh really? Threatened by my even *writing this down*? Lame!" In the moment of giving myself freedom to express, I know I am approaching my most powerful truth.

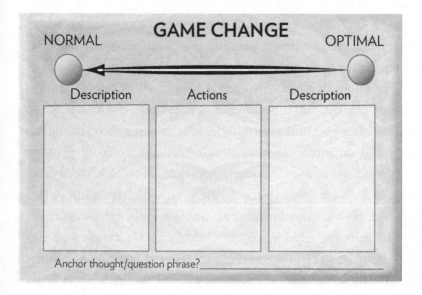

In the same way that your habituated self is sometimes tempted to deny dreams or invalidate accomplishments—yours and those of others—it may, as you begin identifying aligned actions, try to tug you backward. Don't swim in that polluted river. This urge to shut off the process of identifying aligned actions may show up in the form of a grammatical or literary critique of your choice in words, a voice inside your head saying, "This is stupid." Or the creativity-killing effect of feeling as if there's a stopwatch tracking how long the process is taking you. Keep writing. Forget logistics or viability, feasibility, money, childcare, writing ability, etc. and just keep writing.

You have to look carefully at the whole of your life for clues as to what those dream-aligning activities may be. Many lists begin with things folks remember doing at another time in their lives that made them feel great. These might include an activity from childhood or college, a dormant hobby, spending time with a certain friend, a solitary activity, or a pastime that helped you to connect with others. Perhaps you loved painting as a kid in art class, but you now walk through the world telling people you're not creative. Maybe after a few champagne toasts at a wedding you find yourself gleefully dancing into the night, while on most other days you heed the voice of protest within you, and if asked, say that you "don't dance." Maybe you find yourself really enjoying spending time with people outside your customary social circle, who have different life experiences or worldviews. Or maybe you are amazed by the peace and clarity you get from being alone. As I describe these scenarios, you no doubt have experiences you love coming to mind, experiences you find it difficult to justify making happen for yourself. Chances are you've never associated them with fulfillment or success. But they are actually essential for helping you access the feelings necessary to lead you toward deep fulfillment.

URGE AUTOPILOT

Most of us have frequent urges to take actions that lie outside our established norms. As you nurture your vision for your Game-Change, you may find that the number of these urges increases. Here's what you need to do: Honor each vision you have of yourself. While walking down a street, if your impulse is to duck into a store, do it. Whether it's a good experience or ho-hum, *Why the hell did I do that?* is not important to ask. It's not about finding a winning lottery ticket lost on the floor within. It's about strengthening your dialogue with your intuition, your own precious impulses. Order what you truly want, say what you really feel...try it and see how you feel as a result.

You'll start to notice yourself gravitating toward beneficial physical activities, social commitments, intellectual curiosities, and personal self-care practices. *The more you connect action to experiential outcome, the more you'll begin to recognize the connectedness of even your smallest choices to your Radical Success in this lifetime.* And yes, I intentionally use that kind of grandiose imagery because that's actually the truth of the matter—this is all about optimizing your state in this lifetime.

If you feel stuck, consider what made you feel restless enough to try this process: Often the very qualities you long to experience are the instigators of brainstorming actions that help you to actually live them. Whatever your catalyst words are, ask yourself to name at least two actions you can write down that would give you greater alignment with those words.

You have already given your Optimal a name, or at least a description—now I want you to start to see it with documentary-like clarity. As you conceive it, remember how you first said you wanted to feel—what is Optimal to you? Imagine feeling that way from the very first moment of a day. Now that you know how you want to feel, what do you imagine someone who feels that way doing?

For me, aligning with my Optimal has meant deciding to take singing lessons every week. It's meant acknowledging that every day around 3PM I need a clarity break, and giving myself just 20 minutes at the time, to clear my mind. It's meant getting up at 5AM to meditate and work out, and at the other end, getting into bed by 10PM, as unglamorous as it may sound. It's meant experimenting with my own life, doing things I never imagined doing: trapeze, triathlons, surfing, and snowboarding. It's meant spending more time alone, playing social butterfly less often. Does this list of relatively small actions sound like such stuff as dreams are made on? I promise you, for me it has been.

For Melanie, the Optimal state of energy she wanted was *vibrant*. Her use of that specific word provided the springboard for asking what makes her feel vibrant. She could see vibrancy in others. She just had to start giving herself permission to be that way. She started by acknowledging that the bike rides she and her husband took together gave her that feeling. She added that getting up early enough (and being sufficiently clear headed) to take a morning walk, along with eating smaller meals, made her feel vibrant. She started with committing to those actions, and quickly the list grew. The more frequently she took actions that made her feel vibrant, the more she could identify other things that would achieve the same result— joining a volleyball team, splitting an entree, chucking her shapeless clothing and splurging on new, sexier duds with the money she saved by eating smaller portions, flirting with her husband...A host of activities quickly unfolded, all because she stayed committed to the concept of *vibrant*. Her loyalty to that feeling allowed her to embody it.

This list of actions you come up with should look both alarmingly on target and slightly logistically impossible. "Alarmingly on target" because it should be loaded with things you say that you want all the time, including some things you've never admitted to wanting to try. When you read it, you should feel like it describes what you would be doing if you lived in a parallel universe where anything is possible. Because that's where you're going to start living—a parallel universe that has been waiting for you all along. This is why it's so important for it to seem a bit impossible according to your old paradigm/ecosystem. If it didn't seem just slightly impossible, I'd tell you it's not a big enough stretch for you, not a marked enough contrast to your current everyday life in order for you to get a payoff in actualizing it. Only by overcoming a healthy sense of fear will you gain a true sense of accomplishment.

LIVE THE DREAM

As you work on cultivating dreams and vision for yourself, try focusing your awareness of how it feels to actually experience your desired state and your desired outcomes. When you imagine yourself achieving or experiencing something you dream of, ask yourself what it would actually feel like by conducting an inventory of all five senses, as well as your imagined emotional state. The power of the sensate creates an anchor that is precognitive. When directed towards cultivating positive feelings, you shift your baseline norm from humdrum to incrementally better each time. This will help you not only to overcome any "change back" impulses you experience, but will help you recognize more skillfully the right course of action in each endeavor.

Sitting with this exercise usually provides enough insight to work with, so that you naturally start making specific commitments—what you're going to do daily, weekly, and monthly. Your desired states are your benchmark. Continually referring back to them will help you evaluate whether those actions indeed give you the payoff you had wanted, or if you need to modify or change them entirely. These are your process goals. With ongoing attention and pruning, in time they actually *are* the change you wish to see and feel.

When looking at this list, it's useful to break these actions down according to size. Which are *tweaks* (little changes to preexisting routines/actions)? Which are *steps* (moderate commitments that will involve a new behavior or action)? And which are *leaps* (something never before considered that will impact many other routines)? This breakdown will provide some metrics to apply, so you can notice how much effort you're exerting for each. Some of these may fall into an obvious category. Some may seem like they could fit into any of the three, depending on what kind of day you're having and what your attitude is.

American society critiques itself as being overly motivated by instant gratification. But instant gratification isn't all bad. Feeling better in ways you have always wished to feel is an extremely powerful instant reward for taking actions that align you with your Optimal. Think about that. If an action aligns, notice feeling better for having aligned, congratulate yourself, celebrate, and most of all, let it be gratifying. With practice, paying attention to how you feel in the moment becomes your guiding determinant for how you think, what actions you undertake, what you say, and how, when, and where you redirect thoughts and actions.

Remember this important insight: Oftentimes, when transforming your initial catalyst list into your epic action agenda, there will be desired states you aren't quite sure how to achieve. You won't yet know which actions will bring about the qualities you want. Don't worry. That's normal. In fact, it's good. Those qualities are usually ones you haven't really explored much in the past, or have a hard time imagining working into your life. That's okay—clearly those qualities were precluded by the convictions of your old life, or they wouldn't stump you. What stumps you is usually where the potential for breakthrough lies. Entertain the possibility that thoughts are mutable, that you are just a bundle of energy with some established patterns, and that there are always other patterns to be created. Taking that perspective gives you permission to believe that these as-of-yet action-less qualities are still possible for you to embody. These qualities are associated with your big leap, your Holy Grail. Whatever you didn't come up with a certain action for is now the experimentation point, and signifies where you should dig deeper. Whatever stumps you offers you the greatest potential for learning and evolution— and might surprise you in ways you can't anticipate.

Get ready to rumble.

Alignment Assignment

1. Choose to adopt one action that feels like a little *tweak,* and one that is a solid *step.* Even if they are adjustments to what you already do in the course of your day or week, commit to them.

2. Take on a single *leap!* It may require research, getting support from others, etc., but definitely set it in motion this week.

3. Notice how you feel when you adopt these new alignment initiatives, no matter how big or how small. What is the payoff for your inner state? How do others around you respond?

4. How do you respond when others around you change?

Part 3
GAME ON

Chapter 7

WHAT WILL HAPPEN
IF I FAIL?

To someone living and thriving in their Optimal state, everything that happens is part of the aggregate lesson.

Failure? Well, it is inherent in learning any lesson. Failure is a part of success.

Game-Changing requires ongoing course-correction, not instant perfection. If you've decided failure at any point is not an option, why even bother trying? Those curveballs, the ones that life tosses your way? They'll happen. A meeting will run late when you had planned on going to the screenwriting class. A contract will contain clauses to which you cannot agree. Your partner, friend, or colleague will show an aspect of him/herself you struggle to accept. Or perhaps you will succumb to a "venting" session so sodden with negativity that crawling home to a hot shower (or a shot of tequila) feels like the only remedy. You Game-Change the moment you become present to the situation exactly as it is, aware of your options, and from there choose the path most resonant with the person you want to be.

Curveballs happen to the best of us, and perhaps by no coincidence, often at the least opportune moments.

Keith was a bright-eyed professional. Still in the early days of his career, he instinctively knew he had the right stuff to make the C-suite one day. He wanted to accomplish this, but worried about doing so with his passion for life intact. With three young children at home (including newborn twins), he could already feel his responsibilities dampening his enthusiasm. As much as he loved his family and work, handling it all was already feeling like too much, and he noticed that the guys at the office who were twice his age looked brittle and burned-out. Keith wasn't willing to emulate their example and lose himself along the way. Fortunately, he could very easily envision a greater sense of connectedness to himself. But between attending classes to complete his MBA a few nights a week and helping his wife with commitments at home, he didn't have or see any wiggle room. As if on cue, just as Keith began engaging in Game-Change, his boss added to his load by handing him a high-profile project, one that would usually have gone to someone with twice his years of experience. It took Keith off course. Confirming his old convictions about the incompatibility between success and satisfaction, he instinctively started to pull away from his Optimal. Positing he had to choose between relative accomplishment and Radical Success, Keith was cowing to the reactive fear that optimizing would compromise his ability to succeed with the new project. As the venerated flow-guru, U of Chicago psychology head Mihaly Csikszentmihalyi puts it, "When people restrain themselves out of fear, their lives are by necessity diminished. Only through freely chosen discipline can life be enjoyed and still kept within the bounds of reason."

The take away? The minute you think of quitting is the very moment that you need to hang on. You shouldn't quit so easily. As Keith experienced, there is never an easy time to take on cultivating a greater relationship with life—the only perfect time to do so is right now. Dealing with logistical conundrums and best-laid plans gone awry offers a real test in overcoming the fears and insecurities that opposition triggers deep inside us. To navigate whatever life throws your way, you have to get back on track, not by making these issues go away, but activating your Game-Change right now, even with life conditions *exactly as they are.* Being confronted by challenging circumstances doesn't indicate that the process hasn't worked; it indicates that it's time to put the process to work. Life will give you plenty of opportunities for practice, and in Keith's case, the added pressure from the new project provided him with just what he needed to prove to himself those old convictions were dead wrong.

Curveballs that are thrown at you while your old normal is still pretty fresh and your Game-Change is just starting to show results, can provide a prime opportunity to manage that old limiting voice. There are several ways to defuse this mistaken but practiced voice. One powerful tool is interwoven throughout this little book in the form of your Alignment Assignments—they are "walking-around attention practices," designed to help you break up your old ways of perceiving the world, and to help you use elements in your everyday life as your anytime/every time teacher. Presence and conscious observation of the world around you allow you to become more aware of your own mindset, and the ways in which your patterns might be bringing you way, way down.

ARE YOU THRIVING?

Another powerful way to conquer that old voice is by acknowledging your own capacity to align in any situation. Alignment isn't just that surging feeling you get when things go your way, or when everything converges in such a way that things go even better than expected. Alignment doesn't occur simply in the vacuum of obstacles. It means living your Game-Change so you can thrive in any context, no matter what it may be. "Thrive" means to flourish, prosper, or grow. It makes no reference to the level of ease in which such flourishing may be accomplished. In fact, the oldest recorded meaning attributed to the word is "To grasp firmly to oneself." Doesn't that sound amazing? Beyond any external condition, *thriving* is the sublime state of you being resolutely *you*. Notice that the definition isn't dependent upon what your living circumstances are, whether the kids behaved at breakfast, how much money you make, whether you had sex this morning, or how good it was if you did.

If you take a lesson from nature and pay attention to the etymology of the word, thriving is nothing more than feeling like your undistracted self, at peace, at home. Feeling this way as frequently and as consistently as possible is a perfect baseline goal to reach for. For one thing, it's free.

For another, it's a state to be achieved independently of external circumstances. What's more, it's gender-, class-, genus-, and species-neutral. An ant can thrive as certainly as an armadillo, an oak tree, or a CEO.

The general quality of your state of being is often measured by how many moments you can cite feeling positive. As you mine through your data bank, such moments can include times when things have gone right, instances in which people have celebrated and valued your gifts, and moments when the experiences you've dreamed of have unfolded beautifully. These are helpful memories to use in shaping your experience of being alive. But even more helpful is remembering times when you simply felt a heightened sense of being at peace, completely independent of any external affirmation or validation. You have to look for evidence of your ability to feel at peace in the world, and begin to train yourself to use your inherent power to *thrive* no matter the circumstances, especially as you seek to create new, better realities in life.

So when was the last time you thrived? You reinforce your capacity to thrive by remembering instances in which you have experienced it. If you're having a tough time answering that question, how about this one? Name a moment when you felt fully yourself, completely at peace, and in harmony with the world around you. Memories may include moments as seemingly insignificant as having parked the car, and then feeling peaceful in the silence before you disembarked on your next commitment. They may include a time when you found yourself looking earnestly into someone's eyes. One senior executive cited a moment in the midst of hectic business travel when she inadvertently made eye contact with a stray kitten she passed in the street. That seemingly mundane, everyday experience put her at peace and reminded her of her own humanity. Another client recalled when, years before, as an aspiring young professional rushing to a business lunch, he caught and broke the heel of one of his cheap loafers on the doorjamb as he entered the restaurant. He had been worried about his ability to perform well in his new role, but this minor gaffe took him off guard, in a good way. He found himself laughing so hard with the maître d'hôtel that he forgot about his performance anxiety. He walked into the meeting in a state of utter calm.

My own "go-to moments" are deceptively simple—almost absurdly so. They include a time when I was late for an international flight at Atlanta's sprawling Hartsfield airport, rushing from a taxi to the gate. Mid-concourse, a skycap appeared and smiled at me through mirrored shades. He nodded slightly. "Alright," he said. "You're okay, sis." And I was calmed. I use that memory to remind myself even now, years later, that I'm always okay.

But the memory I have used most consistently to generate a sensation of ease in myself is one of a random fall day when I was around five years old playing alone on a playground. I remember it being a beautifully sunny morning. My dad, a Montessori teacher, was inside the adjacent school at a meeting. Something about the experience of being on the swings, swinging alone, feeling the air on my skin, smelling the pine needles, enjoying the quiet, and observing the brilliance of the light, filled me with a deep knowing that I was connected effortlessly to life. Truth.

Another moment I refer to occurred after I ditched my university studies for an unpaid internship. It was with a grassroots service organization, and meant months away from paid work—a tough trade-off for a student loan-saddled sophomore. While walking into that office for the first time, I noticed the leaves on the trees around the brick structure. Something in that moment reminded me that life unfolds with grace—as has all my time spent with that organization, one I still work with to this day.

Can remembering something as simple as feeling deeply okay decrease our anxiety? Can that memory of me as a five-year-old playing on a fall day disempower distracting, unproductive fears around money, self-worth, and my ability to navigate tough decisions? You betcha. Can recalling a moment of insight about life's unfolding serve me now? Without a doubt. I've used both while in meetings, when I've felt old fears begin rising up. I've used them at times when I've suddenly found myself in conflict with friends. I've used them to calm myself while speaking in front of live television cameras. I've used these and other examples when weighing important choices impacting many areas of my life.

Trust me on this: The more often you use your memories of moments of ease, of thriving, the stronger a resource they become. The more you recognize evidence of your own ability to be at peace in the world, the more you will disarm feelings of dismay about how things might have gone in the past and fears about how things might still go in the future. You'll be able to disrupt stressful moments when you're too concerned about others' feelings toward you. When you operate from an established state of equanimity, you're less likely to repeat fear-based patterns that keep you unconsciously chained to old experiences and outcomes. By repeatedly referencing your ability to thrive, you cognitively reinforce a powerful neurological pathway to freedom and peace.

SENSATIONAL NOW

Whenever you find yourself with a moment of suspended action—waiting for a meeting to begin, standing in line to board an airplane, killing time while your computer boots up, or even waiting to be served at a restaurant—rather than digging for your smartphone, try this mastery alternative:

- Observe the physical reality. Notice where you are positioned in space, in relation to your surroundings—details such as furniture and people. As a scene in a movie, allow your awareness to draw out of yourself, and observe the totality of the setting.
- Observe the colors. What are the colors around you? How do they combine?
- Observe textures. Are the surfaces smooth or velvety? Rough or dirty? Just notice.
- Observe the temperature, now the light—its angle and sources.
- Observe the sounds you hear—draw each and every one into your awareness and notice how you respond to them.

Were there any surprises? Think about how you might apply this into every moment of your life.

This isn't merely a distraction tactic. It's also a rewiring tactic, making this a two-pronged strategy. What do you do when a baby is feeling discomfort? You remedy the situation by picking it up and comforting it. What do you do to shift a pet's attention? You toss a bone to distract it. What do you do when a friend is sad? You remind them of all that is good in the world, thereby redirecting their awareness to a better perspective, i.e., giving them something to think about that is more aligned with their well-being. What do amazingly accomplished people do on a daily basis? Reflect upon accomplishments that foster a sense of gratitude, i.e., refocus attention away from limiting thoughts.

Keith used these tactics. He remembered his greatest moments of peace. Looking at thumbnail descriptions he'd put together of a handful of peak moments, he was able to easily recognize that there were elements of both order and nature in them. In alignment with his process goals, and honoring his love of order, he and his wife rented a full-sized dumpster one weekend, and purged their home of every shred of clutter. To maintain the new sense of order, they agreed to eat out less often and allocated the money instead for a cleaning service. They bought all-terrain jogging strollers for the new little ones, so Keith could take the twins on a jog through their neighborhood park each morning while his wife got the toddler ready for preschool. To give himself an outcome goal, he signed up for a muddy trail race, and he went for the full 10K. What's more, to keep himself feeling orderly and grounded internally, he took on the practice of nightly reflection with his wife, each of them committing to sharing three observations of good fortune/gratitude to complete their day. Taking these small strides was part of Keith's baseline commitment to remaining connected with himself, to begin and end each day with a sense of thriving.

Life changes are generated in one of two ways: internally or externally. Changes generated internally usually involve choices you make. Those generated externally tend to be spurred by circumstances you encounter. They're not entirely separate, though. Each has repercussions on the other. Generating intentional change from within is tricky in ways that responding to external factors isn't. With internally generated changes you have to summon courage, creativity, and determination in order to resist the temptation to go back to being how you were. Because these changes require you to demand more for yourself and from yourself, it can be very easy to cheat on satisfying your own needs. But your own needs are exactly what prepare you to effectively work with everything else you encounter in life. What's more, in skillfully generating intrinsic change, you amplify your ability to align your responses to extrinsic impetuses for change, which helps you to achieve Radical Success.

By mining your life for golden moments of thriving, you elicit evidence from your own experience that the way you want to be is undeniably possible because you have already been that way many, many times. In the case of Keith, focusing on what he needed to feel clear and empowered evoked a new image of himself, a new possibility even when his immediate circumstances challenged him. It can work for you, too. If you apply this in your present moments, you disarm the fear response that might otherwise take hold of you and ultimately shut down your efforts toward acting in support of your Optimal self.

By paying attention to just how often you are actually

doing fine, you have an opportunity to overcome your habits of agonizing over the past, prognosticating doom into the future, or finding fault with life in general. It can be surprising as you start to notice that there are far more moments in your day-to-day life in which you *do* experience a state of happiness or ease. The more you remember and value these historic moments of thriving, the more aware you will be of how often this is actually your state in everyday life. Realizing that you have the capacity to be happy without any special situation happening, without any prescribed set of boxes being checked or accomplishment being achieved, is a key to freedom and power, to thriving no matter what is going on around you. Armed with such insight, you can get on with enjoying your life.

Remember: It's all target practice. And practice makes perfect.

Alignment Assignment

1. You've had some high holy moments—ones of ease and peace in your life. I'm not talking about moments like winning the Oscar. I'm talking about those experiences of deep, almost unimaginable well-being. Things might have even been going wrong during one of those moments—no judgment there. Just see if you can first call up one or two memories that really remind you of that state, then dig for as many additional ones as possible.

2. Practice going there *frequently*. When sitting at the doctor's office. When waiting for a meeting to start. When your mom is being a nag. When you feel like running out of a party where you don't know anyone.

3. Start noticing how often you are thriving. Maybe it's while walking from your car to the office. Maybe it happens as you are looking at labels in the grocery store. Begin to notice how often you are actually in a state of complete harmony.

4. Keep your eyes open to ways other people thrive. Notice, when you are around others, whether they seem to give off a sense of well-being, contented empowerment, or peace. Listen to how they speak about their lives. What is "normal" to them? What can you learn from them?

Chapter 8

WHAT IF EVERYONE THINKS I'M CRAZY FOR DOING THIS?

Are you a sheep or a lion? Are you willing to focus for the rest of your life upon conditioned and conventional preoccupation with physical safety and status issues, or are you ready to skillfully project the whole ball of wax of who you are onto what truly fulfills you? In any moment, you can opt for what most allows you to protect and remain the person you have cultivated yourself to be, or for what most allows you to grow to encompass not only your external trappings of success, but to include and be enhanced by the experiences that feed your being as well.

In the previous chapter you played with recalling peak moments, a powerful tool to use when encountering logistical and practical difficulties along the path toward Radical Success. Aside from the inevitable challenges of timing and happenstance, the most powerful mitigating factors in making life changes often come in the form of well-intended (and sometimes not so well-intended) people around you. *Tread bravely.*

In the face of these behavioral shifts, not only do you each have to confront your own discomfort and unfamiliarity with new choices, but you have to also deal with the "change back" messages you get from loved ones, colleagues, and associates. This is serious stuff, because these messages can cause the human nervous system to send a bevy of fear-response chemicals surging throughout the body, making you think that if you act in your own best interest, the tribe or pack is going to send you out into the tundra alone – ultimately to your death. The primordial survival instinct, which is usually referred to as common sense, has taught you to fear this.

The additional pressure of "change back" messages resulting from the discomfort of others requires a different type of discipline and determination than adapting to life's curveballs does. Remember: As you increasingly align with what you really want in life, the more oppositional certain situations, ways of thinking, and conversations may feel. In Game-Change, your strongest course is to embrace each obstacle as part of your success.

Ironically you can experience this strong opposition even from the people who have the most to gain from your new way of being. For example, sixty pounds lighter and having traveled a quarter of the way toward his goal, Jeff had a perfect test in staying true to his Game-Change. Just as he sat down after a late evening workout to enjoy a lean cut of meat and hearty salad for dinner, his wife demanded he immediately stop, get in the car, and drive to McDonald's to pick up food for the rest of the family. Never mind that by making his hard-won changes, Jeff had aligned with his intention to be around longer as a good financial provider, husband, and father. Never mind that what his wife was asking was the equivalent of asking a recovered junkie to make a drug run. This is just one example of how people around you can find lots of ways to show you they are really frightened of change. From any direction, at times you might get so heavily whacked with what is not Optimal, that it's easy to forget your dreams are possible at all.

LIKE ME

While in a public place with lots of people, practice the following and notice what occurs. As you look at individuals, repeat the following to yourself:

- Like me, this person is seeking some happiness for his/her life.
- Like me, this person is trying to avoid suffering in his/her life.
- Like me, this person has known sadness, loneliness, and despair.
- Like me, this person is seeking to fulfill his/her needs.
- Like me, this person is learning about life.

The biggest hurdle you may encounter in achieving your Game-Change may be that others don't know how to respond when you start behaving in ways you never have before. The steak-and-potatoes guy is hitting the sushi line? It can be a social confrontation, and I mean that in all seriousness. Take what happened when Alissa, every-one's favorite "last-call-for-alcohol" girl, called it a night at 10PM, heading home to drink water and go to bed. Her behavior was so shocking to her friends that Alissa was persuaded to give up on herself. Judgmental glances, cold shoulders, and snide remarks from "friends" may not seem like heavy artillery, but from a social perspective, they are just that. Alissa and others may give up on themselves, but using the tools you're about to explore, you'll see that you don't have to. After this chapter you'll know how, in the midst of change, your mind *is* the leavening agent. Let's look at how to use it to lighten things up and enlighten your thinking.

Succumbing to unconscious fear about these tiny shifts is the biggest risk against achieving Radical Success. I've seen more people cop out, roll up the sidewalk, and go back to whatever they used to consider home because of peer pressure, or rejection from their social set—in some cases just the fear of it—than any other causes. The party girl I mentioned above, a talented young woman in her late twenties, withdrew from the Game-Change process because she wasn't willing to give up her custom of late night socializing with chicken wings and beer in order to be more clear and efficient at work, and have more energy and self-esteem. Never mind that all she would have had to do is manage her choices differently. I saw a married father of two quit his mid-six-figure job as chief financial officer of a small medical devices company during a depressed economy over a simple misunderstanding at work, rather than consider that his need to be seen as perfect was getting in his way.

The unconscious experience of seeking approval has the power to drive your every moment. It's simply wired into your survival instinct. We all experience this need to belong, and we each give it expression in our own way. Think of a pack of animals in the wild—an animal is going to want to know that he/she is either strong enough to win, or liked enough to be protected. Every action is calculated based upon his or her understanding of these ever-shifting rankings of strength and popularity. You are no different. You simply have different metrics of validation, and use different skills to secure it.

You might already be aware of this need for approval. Cool! It's just as likely that you find offensive the notion that you base your actions upon how you think others will respond. "But wait," an indignant voice within you may protest. "I don't really care what so-and-so thinks of me. They are so _____ (some disparaging term)— why would I care?" When you couch your relationship to others in a way that protects your rank, you pander to insecurity around validation and belonging. Translated, this could read: *I am so much better; they don't matter.* In this way you protect your superiority, through comparing, right-making, wrong-making, or constant evaluation. The underlying motivation for this evaluation is *still* to affirmatively answer the question: "Am I safe in the pack?"

There's nothing inherently wrong with this. Again, it's driven by the very nervous system responses that kept your ancestors from going extinct. The problem is that it costs too much. It squanders energy in the form of thoughts and actions that do nothing to advance you toward achieving your Optimal state. It locks you into the false assumption that whatever is okay with the pack defines success for yourself, rather than determining your game on your own terms. It keeps you living in a false paradigm of having to protect yourself socially, to survive by conforming down to even the most mundane choice. Again, as U Chicago's

Csikszentmihalyi said, "When people restrain themselves out of fear, their lives are by necessity diminished. Only through freely chosen discipline can life be enjoyed and still kept within the bounds of reason."

GROUNDING BREATH

A major contributor to your sense of well-being is the sympathetic nervous system—the system that generates responses such as "fight or flight" and "tend and befriend." Built to identify both opportunities and threats, this system can often shift into overdrive with the overwhelming number of perceived opportunities and challenges that arise through the course of a given day. Whenever you notice signs of anxiety or find yourself feeling less than centered or grounded, do the following to support your sympathetic nervous system:

- Soften your eyes, tongue, and jaw.
- Inhale deeply so that you feel your belly expand. Then, exhale with the same attention to your abdomen.
- As you repeat this breathing exercise, notice if your inhale is shorter than your exhale or vice versa.
- Begin to even out the length of your inhale and exhale.

Lives diminished. Sound yucky? It is. *And it's completely optional.* That's right. Even though the human nervous system has been responding to stimuli in this conditioned way ever since before the discovery of fire, you can consciously short-circuit this mechanism to free up all that energy and begin to make all those choices for yourself, even if it will be for the first time ever.

Take heart. By becoming a keen observer of your

own fear reflexes in response to your perceived social standing, you become free and powerful, and have the opportunity to align your choices. The best way to do this is to catch yourself in the habit of comparative thinking and validation addiction, and to become really good at disentangling yourself from both of these mechanisms. Your challenge is not to necessarily undo all your habits, but to be consciously aware of them and to manage them through cause and effect, action, and outcome.

COMPARE AND DESPAIR

Comparative thinking is any thought about your experience of others that involves evaluative ranking back to yourself. It's the old, *"I win, you lose. You win, I lose."* This may take the form of thoughts like the one I referenced above: "So-and-so is such a _____ (disparaging word)—I'm so much better." Or it could take the form of a positive thought about someone else, followed by a backhanded whack on the back to your own head, e.g., "X-person is so _____ (positive word)—I'm just not as good." It can include a positive estimation of oneself designed to diminish others. Put simply, it's anything that involves a system of ranking yourself in relationship to others. It destroys authenticity in relationships, and locks you into eternal power-jockeying.

Validation addiction shows up any time you take action or share ideas or experiences so that you can get a pat on the back. Oh, I know, it just feels so good! I'm a recovering pat-on-the-back-aholic, myself. And the reason it feels so good is because of that nervous system, which has wired itself to flood yummy friendship-associated chemicals such as endorphins, oxytocin, and progesterone throughout the body whenever you feel safe, even if cognitively you don't completely trust it. If you didn't get addicted to those good feelings, you wouldn't be human.

This is the power of association. To your nervous system, the pat on the back means: "The pack won't abandon me. The chemicals released tell your body: "Hey, everything is okay now—you can relax." We each release these chemicals in different quantities and with different levels of awareness of the ease—feelings of warmth, peace, and receptivity—they create. You may experience them as a slowing in the rhythm of your breath, an easing of the tension in your muscles, or a general sense of peace that spreads throughout your body. No matter how aware of these body chemicals you have been up until now, as you learn to pay attention you'll begin to observe the power of approval and a sense of safety.

Validation addiction can take the form of listening to a group conversation and focusing on nothing but finding a way to insert your two cents. It can include making sure people know of your authority or expertise with respect to a given topic. It can also take the form of giving approval to others in order to feel safer around them or to get them to feel safer around you—this currying favor in order to feel safe is a classic case of "tend and befriend" gone terribly awry. It is driven by a fear that who you are and what you know aren't relevant to a conversation or other moment of engagement, you are somehow irrelevant or unimportant to the pack, and therefore unsafe.

These behaviors are desperate attempts to manipulate opinions, power plays underscoring the misbelief that if you're not angling for safety and acceptance, you're bound to be at risk. They drain your mental focus and capacity. Chemically, they keep you hooked on the influence of the endlessly shifting balance of good-feeling chemicals in response to anxiety-producing chemicals. None of this is inherently negative—it's not a bad thing for folks to feel safe around you. But it certainly isn't good when you prioritize their safety over making choices that align with your Radical Success.

Why does all this matter in terms of realizing your Radical Success? Because your established social norms are the biggest obstacles to your Game-Change. Status quo mechanisms to keep yourself safe and advance your current social standing are your ultimate enemy. You cannot achieve what you want without disentangling from these well-worn assumptions and strategies. Change is the biggest threat to the pack—any pack. A shift will be experienced by the others, even if the change you make is as subtle as going home earlier, moving conversations on to new topics, or ordering salad instead of fries. And yes, even such minor adjustments are change moments, and can prompt negative "change back" reactions.

These moments of discomfort are your training ground for weaning yourself from validation and/or ranking. This is your Game-Changing moment. Even as you're making the smallest of choices, you must cultivate the habit of recognizing these primordial ingrained fear responses, and practice shifting your attention to your own experiential payoff. Instead of gauging your power or popularity via a system of ranking yourself with other people, what if you were to instead gauge, measure, and value your sense of connection to your Optimal self, in everything you do?

Jeff did. He wasn't ready for World War III with his wife, and sensed he had many more options than resorting to anger or victim-thinking. While en route to the McDonald's, Jeff reflected upon the deep fears his wife must be feeling and how they triggered his own fears about their relationship. Rather than plotting to change her or make her wrong, he shifted his attention to the sensation of getting on a treadmill and the moment when the sweat begins to drip from his nose. He literally felt the corner of his mouth turning upward in a peaceful smile as he drove. His breath slowed and changed in rhythm from jagged to easy in, easy out. When the cashier passed the order to him through the drive-thru window, he was surprised at how the smell of the fast food, which he had once considered a normal meal option, now made him nauseated. Sitting in the car at a red light, he realized how far he had already come and laughed. In this moment, he recognized his freedom to align his thinking and his actions, and to allow his wife to wrestle with her own demons and meanwhile lovingly stay his course. He felt an incredible sense of his power to make himself happy, no matter the circumstance. That night as he slept: Jeff dreamed he was at a healthy weight, full of energy, and happy, something he had never seen or imagined before.

The moment of vulnerability and discomfort when you feel the strangeness of new choices can be a moment of sublime power. Maybe you can imagine the rush of adrenaline you might feel when, even in a drunken state, you summon the wisdom to align with your Optimal self and actually order a soda water instead of a third shot of tequila. Maybe your adrenaline-releasing moment would come about while telling your life partner you want to go back to school, dive into a start-up, or that you need support to allocate time to take up a new interest. Prepare yourself by adding to that visualization the "change back" response you might face, whether delivered through an argument or as a joke. Think of it as the discomfort of another person in response to a new choice—it is simply energy. If you can observe it, shut off the primordial fear narrative (e.g., they won't love me, or I'll never fit in again, etc.), and just feel the charge of your own empowered autonomy—your own power to *choose*. Note that as a payoff in and of itself. That's an addiction worth having.

Alignment Assignment

1. Notice your comparative thoughts in every venue of your life—with close companions, colleagues, and even with strangers. Notice how often you make yourself right and others wrong. Notice how much energy you waste in this evaluative black hole.

2. Notice your response in social interactions. How does it feel when others engage on a topic and you have nothing to offer? When you have many ideas but are not asked? When you offer ideas or experiences and no one listens? What about when you are really heard and observed—what happens in your body?

3. Observe how often you praise others to win approval from them. How often do you let your experience of receiving compliments from others influence your mood? Do you notice others seeking your approval?

4. Notice what happens when you make even a small choice that aligns with your Optimal self. What happens inside you? If you're with others, how do they respond? Do they notice? If they respond poorly or negatively, notice what happens inside you. Can you recognize their discomfort and still make your empowered choice? How does it feel?

5. Differentiate between the discomfort that comes with breaking from your habituated desire for approval and/or safety, and the effort necessary for being radically successful.

Chapter 9

HOW DO I KEEP MY FAITH?

Faith is key. By faith I don't mean religion, or belief in a deity, although those forms of faith can be powerful in supporting Game-Change. But by faith I mean conviction in and connection to the function of life itself. We all have faith—it's why you get out of bed in the morning. It's why you eat. Faith is why, despite times in which perhaps you don't want to get out of bed or eat, somehow you eventually rise and nourish yourself again. You have faith that these things are necessary and worthwhile. While certainly religious faith can be a support for your sense of connectedness to life, it's not a requirement.

Faith in life itself is different from blind faith, because you do have proof of the evolutionary power of life. You can observe evidence of that power, of fulfillment and of freedom of choice, by observing your own life, nature, and the lives of countless people around you. The issue isn't whether you *have* faith, but of how frequently you invoke it in support of your own desires. Rather than looking to your fears and doubts to arrange your life, use faith as the organizing principle it can be. Faith is a tool; invoke it.

Philosopher and coach Hugo Cory, a deeply influential force in my understanding of consciousness and optimization, pointed out that once you acknowledge what you want, your thoughts, feelings, words, and actions must align with that desire. It follows to ask, if I say I want to be successful and I define what success is for me, why would I allow my thoughts, feelings, words, or actions to do anything *other* than align with being successful? A truly successful person will manage their mind so that counterproductive processes are not given an opportunity to take root. When you catch yourself thinking or acting counter to your success, you must immediately redirect your thinking to be in alignment with it.

Try this: Name a goal. Let's say you want to be the absolute best you can be at what you do. Maybe currently you're pretty good, but you want to take yourself to the highest level. You can imagine being *that* good—so maybe the idea looks like this:

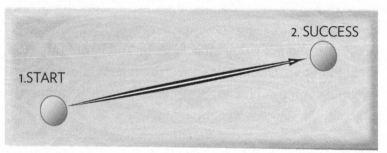

How consistently do your thoughts align with being at your very best? Seriously. How frequently are your thoughts absolutely related to your highest state? How about your habits? How many of them are centered, wastefully, on considering, critiquing, or judging others? Pandering to old patterns? Worrying about the future? Critiquing whatever is happening around you? Putting yourself down? How many of your actions involve either magnifying your own importance to others, or investigating how popular you are on Facebook? Each time you engage in this behavior, you completely squander yourself.

The good news is that this situation is instantly recoverable. All you have to do is redirect those thoughts.

Whether you consider this a leap of faith or simple science, realize that your bandwidth is all you've got. You are bundles of energy, pure and simple, with a central nervous system to direct the energy and a musculoskeletal system to execute its bidding. What if achieving your best possible use of your mind and your efforts (i.e., what you call "life") is as simple as directing yourself wholly to what you decide is best?

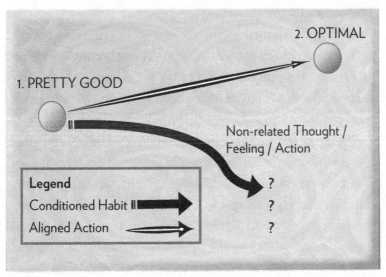

That's the *great* news: The more you catch yourself engaged in non-related thoughts/feelings/actions and learn from doing so, the more you understand your habits, and can redirect and repurpose the amazing bandwidth of potential that is *you*.

Based on the tools you've explored so far, you've learned a lot about having faith, paying attention, and redirecting. You know that most of your self-limiting actions are an innocent response to natural survival fears and the instinct to cultivate safety. There's no fault in that, but there is also little that is productive about those actions.

YOU'VE GOT THE POWER

Maybe you've taught yourself that you're powerless over a habit. In truth, though, your powerlessness can't be farther from the truth. In fact, the greatest power you have is the power to observe and direct your thoughts. The antidote for this misconception of powerlessness is choosing an aligned point of attention. In this chapter you're going practice focusing upon thoughts and engaging in actions that align with your own definition of being successful—not relationally or competitively, but purely in terms of how you cultivate this life force that is *you*.

Getting it straight means invoking your faith. You do this by remembering what you really want at all times. It means valuing your highest good above all else. It means understanding that you can't get to "heaven" if your mind, feelings, thoughts, words, and actions are in your own hellish gutter. It means that you close the time loop between yourself and some distant aspiration. You dispose of any notion of a fairy godmother (someday in the non-specified future) coming and tapping you with a magic wand to make you into the version of yourself most worthy of your respect, and begin to embody that person in all you do *starting right now*.

Because here's the thing: You can't wait for the life you

want, the way you want it, to just magically occur. You have to begin to embody that way of living in every single moment you can. That said, you have to become acutely aware of the mind-bombs in your life—the conversations, activities, and habits that blow your mind from aligning with how and who you want to be, into the state of mind of whoever you've already spent enough time being.

MIRROR, MIRROR

Look at your face closely in a mirror. Observe as a child or a stranger might, and do not let judgments or thoughts about yourself cloud your vision. Just watch. Notice signs of joy, struggle, yearning, strength and emotion that appear in your face as you gaze at it. Relax. Don't stare or make faces. Who do you see? Who is behind or inside your eyes? What changes happen as you look? Notice the fine physical details of your face in a way you never have before. What happens when you simply see yourself? What happens when you judge what you see? What happens when you see yourself with your heart?

Whatever these life-stranglers are, you have to identify them and when you encounter them, correct your course so that you can reclaim yourself from unconscious habit. Mind-bombs and time-bombs: Both annihilate your potential, sending you into a downward spiral, blowing countless seconds, minutes, hours, and days that you could instead be using to experience life as you want to. The sooner you recover from these habits, the sooner you can get back on track.

This confrontation with your old patterns supports you in answering this critical, yet simple, question: Is this habit in support of my highest good? In answering, if you find yourself backpedaling about your thoughts, feelings, words, or actions, or making a lot of excuses for them, you know that you're not aligned. If you can answer simply, and are feeling every bit capable of being the superstar you long to be, you know you are aligned.

FAITH AND FORTUNE

What do you believe? Making an inventory of all that you believe is a powerful reminder of what you hold true about life itself, and also what outdated beliefs you need to shed. Take a look at your own list of beliefs and ask yourself which you hold absolutely undeniably true. Which beliefs support you in creating the life you want? Which limit or impede your ability to evolve?

There's a Native American story about two wolves who live inside each human being: One thrives on love, possibility, hope, and all that's good, while the other is a well of negativity, prone to fighting with and hurting others, and generally at odds with the world. An elder Indian teaches his grandson about these two wolves, and how they fight each other. The grandson asks, "Which wolf will win?" The grandfather answers, "The one you feed."

Your thoughts, feelings, and actions *are* the food. As you feed on negativity you can only experience life from a perspective of what is wrong or lacking. As you invoke your faith to feed on hope, love, and possibility, you will experience that which fills you with contentment.

So what are you consuming? What thoughts do you harbor in order to keep the nourishment positive and whole? What actions help you to naturally generate positive thought-food? What conversations stimulate it?

As you become aware of your thoughts as a form of energetic nourishment, and you align every thought to be fully in support of an Optimal state, you may find that being around others is a different experience entirely. People with whom you may have easily spent time prior to taking on these practices may suddenly be difficult to be around. You may find that your motivation for spending time with other people is no longer the need for acceptance, but simply the desire to share the experience of being alive—nothing more, nothing less.

The more you focus on your idea of Radical Success, the more clear it may become that, for many people, conversational interests are defined by a current of negativity. My friend and beloved editor Alice calls these folks "grief vampires." Here's how conversations with them work: I give you some negative observations, you give me negative observations back, and as a result you feel better sharing in your suffering and view regarding how wrong the world is around you, how hard life is. This unconscious, negative social currency does not indicate that those who engage in it are bad people. It doesn't make them beneath your interest or unworthy of your time. It simply means they haven't learned what you are learning, and spending time with them means learning to be with them exactly as they are, without a single critical thought or judgment of them, all while practicing staying true to that which you know aligns with the Game-Change you want.

You will learn to maintain your alignment silently, without preaching or teaching. You will learn to be with others who are in any mental state and in the midst of any default social currency, positive or not. You will feel rich in your own being without validation or energetic compensation from anyone. By practicing independence in simply being, you begin to *be* who and what you most want to be, regardless of external conditions, people, or circumstances.

Practice always begins now.

Alignment Assignment

1. Keep your mind straight. When you engage in any thought, action, or conversation, first remind yourself of your Game-Change.

2. As the thought, action, or conversation unfolds, remind yourself to only act or speak in alignment with that state.

3. Notice when you do not feel aligned with your new "normal," then immediately realign your next thought, word, or action. Remember—this is about managing *yourself*, not others around you.

4. Only offer insight when asked, and when asked, be attentive so that you can assess receptivity. Don't waste your energy on those who are not receptive.

Part 4

PLAYING FOR LIFE

Chapter 10

HOW DO I SUSTAIN THIS WAY OF BEING OVER TIME?

Treat yourself as a source of energetic support. Manage yourself as a precious resource. Know that responsibility for *yourself* precedes any other responsibility.

Since you began Game-Changing, you've probably started feeling absolutely unique, singularly talented, and seriously kick-ass. Like you can do just about anything you set your mind to—and it's true, you can. It's quite likely you've tweaked assumptions about yourself, experienced your relationships with new awareness, and disrupted many of the self-made systems that have kept you trapped in whatever was before. Congratulations! Now to take on the real challenge—sustaining this level of engagement with possibility. The reason I call this a "challenge" is that you're hard-wired to do the bare minimum, to create a normal that keeps you from dying, and then sustain it. That was true before you took on Game-Changing, and it's true now.

In considering how you keep yourself on track, it's important to bear in mind one discovery about the human mind/body dynamic, and two natural laws. Regarding the mind/body dynamic, you are engineered to conserve energy. In thought, in physical action, in literally every type of energetic expenditure, as a bundle of energetic impulses we are all hoarders, expending only what our instincts tell us is absolutely necessary, not a bit more. In his powerful book *Spark*, Dr. John Ratey of Harvard University uses both historical and neurophysical findings to show that in alignment with our fear-orientation, humans are essentially energy conservers. This is readily reinforced by two basic natural laws usually taught in high school Science 101:

1. **Entropy**

2. **Symbiosis**

Entropy says that the universe reaches a state of homogeneity energetically. Symbiosis says that coexisting systems are interdependent. These two laws basically provide a scientific heads up that rust never sleeps—trending toward sameness is the natural position, so you have to keep cultivating yourself as a way of life. *Holler!* If coasting and conserving for fear of attack is your tendency and complacency is your drive, then you've got to be on guard against regressing. How do you remain engaged in authentic living if your brain is wired to conserve energy, create safety, and generally make sure you don't extend one iota of effort that's more than necessary?

You can count on discomfort being generated externally to remind you periodically that you've got to align to remain Optimal. The curveballs life tosses out are going to keep you on your toes in your efforts to remain radically successful. You can also count on feeling normal human

crankiness—or any of its close relatives, such as irritability, boredom, and impatience—as reminders to wake
up and keep your Game-Change alive.

If you acknowledge this natural tendency to check
out anytime you can, it becomes clear there is no "game
over." It never ends. Game-Changing is your constant
task. Given an essentially energy-conservative default
position, you know you have to work with your exertion
aversion by ensuring a baseline of resourcefulness—and
by that I mean *resource full-ness*, making sure your tanks
are replenished regularly so you can catch those curveballs and notice your crankiness. If you were super-
humanly disciplined, this ongoing maintenance would
happen automatically. Since you aren't, you have to work
to skillfully manage yourself, um, basically forever. So for
the purpose of staying on track, I created a Sustainability
Schedule, a little party favor in the form of a grid you'll
see at the bottom of this chapter. Think of it as inner swag.

PUT A TIGER IN YOUR TANK

What if you were to make a list of activities that
replenish your tank? What if you named all the experiences
that foster a deep sense of happiness inside of you? How
many can you list? Whether speaking to small groups of ten
people or auditoriums packed with thousands, I have never
seen more than 20 percent of any audience raise their hands
indicating they can name more than three things that make
them feel true happiness inside. When I ask for a show of
hands to see who can name more than five things, less than 5

percent of the audience makes this claim. For more than ten experiences they know create happiness, there is rarely more than one person with a raised hand. This is not the case when I ask about listing things that result in negativity. That brings a sea of raised hands.

As a devotee of making Radical Success your everyday reality, you must put yourself on a steady experiential diet of what delights you. Make no mistake: This discipline must be kept for biological and neurological reasons. If what currently fills your daily schedule is a whole lot of firefighting to get through the day, mixed in with a significant amount of worrying about the firefighting and getting through the day, you're experiencing a pretty steady sequence of non-Optimal. The more of that you experience, the more difficult it is to believe in an alternative. Once you're convinced this is the only way to be, unless you course-correct, you'll get to feeling like you'd better batten down the hatches, quit, simmer down, and stop yammering on about feeling fully alive. To manage that default response, remember that happiness can only be cultivated in the present moment. Like scientists, you've got to become experts on your own happy. You've got to become curators of your own contentment.

Whether you like to think of your Optimal experiences using terms like *flow*, *vibrant*, *rock star*, or *in the zone*, you're essentially referring to those activities that remind your nervous system that being worried and afraid are not the only options, you don't have to conserve so much energy, and you've got plenty of energy to spare. Looking ahead through the lens of a system that's been replenished, it's easier to see that there's a *liveliness* still available to you in this lifetime. Taking part in these experiences has a curative effect on your body and a calmative and clarifying effect on your mind. It opens you up to creativity and contentment in all venues and endeavors.

What sustains each of us is different. Knowing what uniquely sustains you is necessary for your own thriving. Whatever these actions are, they are your secret sauce, the magic ingredient to you being at your best. In corporate-speak I refer to them as Sustainable Success Practices, but don't be confused by that terminology. Sustainable Success Practices are not some uniform list of life-affirming actions handed down by researchers or other experts. They are a list *you* curate based upon what actions that you know can rejuvenate, enliven, and inspire you. A term like Sustainable Success Practices helps you to recognize the actual value of these practices you often leave to the bottom of your to-do list, and that they are actually non-negotiables of huge importance. Gravitas aside, these actions are little periodic happy pills (though there's no real pill involved), contentment commitments, bliss bombs, or whatever you want to call them. What's important is that you utilize them during your regular day so that you're tipping the balance of your life diet *in favor* of the experience of truly "better" living.

As you work with them in the below chart, you'll see I'm encouraging you to organize your Sustainable Success Practices by time increments. Some activities may take only seconds and be doable just about any time, such as attentively feeling cool water roll down your throat or consciously breathing slowly and deeply. Others, such as spending time with your sketchpad or walking through the park, you may feel are best enjoyed if given twenty minutes or a full hour. Still others may be yummy, once-in-a-lifetime experiences that require a full month, whether it be a trip to Antarctica or a hike along the Appalachian Trail. The more fluent you are in your own sources of happiness at any given moment or in any situation, the more resourceful you will be in using every moment for cultivating contentment, rather than mindlessly surrendering your thoughts to useless concerns. What's more, by recognizing that each of your Sustainable Success Practices bears a different frequency and time commitment, you can both identify the categories in which you might need to find more practices in support of your well-being, and heighten your awareness that your state of well-being is fundamentally and completely in your own hands.

SUSTAINABLE SUCCESS SCHEDULE

Activity/Practice	Ongoing	Daily	Weekly	Monthly	Annual/ Lifetime

Honoring, recognizing, and using these practices results in your heightened ability to shift the ecosystem that is your life from one of surviving to thriving. The term "sustainability" implies prolonged life—important, as whatever lives also dies. Keep the thrive alive. By having chosen to Game-Change the life that is *you* into an *Optimal you*, you've earned the glorious mandate to infuse that life with more

Optimal activities. Rather than simply sustaining a perpetual cycle of half-hearted moments, frustrated desires, fear-based relationships, and soul-negating convictions, make Optimal choices to ensure that the life you're sustaining is truly to your delight. By infusing yourself with Optimal actions, your creativity and sense of possibility will allow continued, fantastic ideas and possibilities to surface, taking your life in wonderful directions you might not otherwise have even allowed yourself to imagine. That is Radical Success.

Sound good?

Welcome to the rest of your optimized life. Take good care of it.

GRATITUDE

Small though this book is, it's the result of loving support, professional skills, and life wisdom imparted by editors, designers, students, teachers, friends, family, and strangers who have helped me along this path.   Without this orchestra of creators to help me, this book would never have happened.

ABOUT THE AUTHOR

Heralded in the bestselling Megatrends 2010 as "corporate mindfulness guru for the new millennium," Tevis Trower has helped a broad range of powerful organizations to optimize their most precious assets: Human Beings. In the process, she is proof that professional accomplishment and happiness are not mutually exclusive.

Prior to her work enhancing corporate and executive performance, Tevis held a number of other occupations and titles. Burger flipping, ditch-digging and community-building in Nicaragua, serving as a U.S. Army Reservist, rising as a deal diva for Fortune 500s, co-Chair of the *New York Yoga Teachers Association*, and advisory board member for the New York Chapter of the American Diabetes Association, Tevis' success is radical, constantly evolving and the embodiment of what she helps others achieve.

With a Master's degree in International Business, Tevis has gleaned wisdom from renowned teachers in a broad selection of leadership and mastery disciplines, including Sally Kempton, Hugo Cory, Sharon Salzberg, Lama Surya Das, as well as MIT professors Peter Senge, Otto Scharmer, and Fred Kofman. She was mentored in innovation, coaching, and group facilitation by Michael Ray, Professor of Creativity and Innovation, and Marketing (Emeritus) at Stanford University's Graduate School of Business.

She has created and facilitated global executive immersions for prestigious organizations including *Harvard Business Review Events, Young Presidents' Organization, PwC, Disney, Morgan Stanley, KKR, Soros, Viacom, Google, NYPD,* and *The Economist Group,* on team effectiveness, organizational engagement, mindfulness, executive lifestyle, personal mastery, innovation, and the role of consciousness in creating radical success.

You can find Tevis featured in respected media outlets such as *Forbes, Fortune, BusinessWeek, Glamour, Yoga Journal, CIO, Pink, Real Simple, Crain's, New York Post, Financial Times, WWD, New York Observer, MSNBC, CNBC, Fox Business, NY1,* and *Martha Stewart* and worklife expert to *WebMD* and the *Huffington Post.*

Living what she teaches, Tevis spends time in NYC, Montauk, and Woodstock, enjoying surfing, snowboarding, trail runs, and entertaining friends at home with her little doggy, Ruby.